The Baby DILEMMA

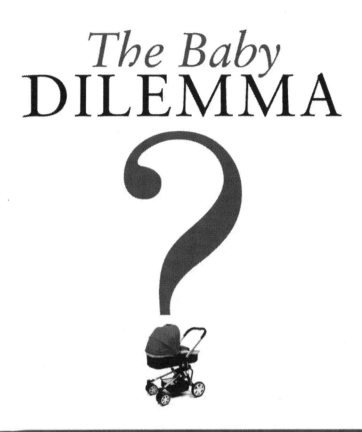

How to Confidently Decide Whether or Not to Have a Child and Feel Good About It

ANN MEREDITH, JD, MBA

The Baby Dilemma
Ann Meredith, JD, MBA

ISBN-13: 978-1492232230
ISBN-10: 1492232238"

Visit www.annmeredith.net for more information about his book and its author. Note: At the request of interviewees, the names and identifying characteristics have been changed to protect their privacy.

DEDICATED TO

Ansen Von Walewander,
who has taught me so much about love.

TABLE OF CONTENTS

INTRODUCTION

I was born in 1965, the year the Supreme Court legalized birth control. I'm not sure if this had anything to do with it, but as I grew up, I never wanted to have children or be married. Although I came from a large extended Catholic family with about 25 first cousins, having children was NOT something I wanted to do. I was more interested in reading, learning, adventure, and travelling the world. So, after high school, I went to college and then to law school. I married a professional baseball player the year I was admitted to practice law, and then pursued my career as he pursued his. I ended up working at the PGA TOUR, Commerce Clearing House, Accenture, Deloitte & Touche, Intel, Gateway, an Internet start-up, Equant and Perkins, Coie. I also obtained an MBA in International Business and lived and worked in Europe and traveled extensively.

During all of that time, I would confidently tell people that I didn't want to have children. However, I struggled internally with that thought. I wondered if there was something wrong with me because I never felt a maternal desire toward children. I didn't like babysitting, although I did enjoy the children I had some kind of connection to, mainly those of friends and family. But, in general, kids were not my thing. Yet, I was married to someone who was patient, kind, and nurturing. He said he didn't want children, either, but was open if I ever changed my mind.

One of the main reasons I didn't want to have a child was that I had a negative view of motherhood. The caretaking of children appeared to consist of a lot of mundane, tedious, boring work and differed from the exciting lifestyle that was my vision of a fulfilling life. My godmother, a family friend, was a woman who didn't – couldn't – have children and ended up going to law school. She worked, travelled, and had freedom to pursue her interests. Her lifestyle seemed more interesting and appealing than staying at home with or raising children.

Another influence in my decision not to have a child was that my mother didn't seem to enjoy motherhood very much. She was an intelligent woman who didn't go to college. After I and then my brother were born, my mother stayed home with us for a few years and then went to work for a stock brokerage company. She was one of the first female brokers at her firm. She worked on and off throughout my younger childhood and continued full time as I started elementary school. And it seemed that she enjoyed working more than she liked being a mom. There wasn't much interest in me or my school work, and I mostly raised myself.

My mother also became a single mother when my parents divorced when I was 13, and then work became a necessity for her. My father, who was a builder and real estate developer, wasn't around much, and I saw that work and a career seemed to offer more stability and a more rewarding future than being with children. My mother also emphasized, "Get an education. No one can take that away from you." She was more concerned that I was self-sufficient and could provide for myself.

But, being married to a loving person for eight years influenced me. I struggled with deciding whether I wanted to have a child. I wanted to make a decision based on my own wants and desires, not one influenced by my childhood experiences. I wanted to make a decision based on the adult person that I had become. And, although my spouse said he didn't want to have a child, I was wondering if he was just doing what I wanted because he cared for me, and that one day he'd regret it.

In order to get some clarity, I started reading all the books that were written about, "How to Decide to Have a Child," and found that there weren't many. The ones that did exist didn't help me sort out my thoughts. Many of the books I found were outdated, written in the 1970s when women were just starting to benefit from feminism and getting more choices in life, and motherhood was attacked as being a less-than-fulfilling option. The authors of those books complained that motherhood had been idolized for too long, making many women who chose that route seem miserable. There were also books written by women who decided not to have children, but their content seemed to justify the position of not having children, rather than provide any method to help someone sort through the issues and their thoughts. In addition, there weren't any books that could give me factual information on important issues and a decision-making process that could help me clarify my position.

I decided to fill that gap and write a book to help me make my decision. I thought that if I sorted through the issues during the writing process, by the end, I would have made my decision. So, besides reading books and doing research, I interviewed people about how they made their decision. I conducted about 300 one-on-one interviews and conducted a 100-person survey. These people came from a wide variety of socio-economic backgrounds and were at different stages of their decision-making process.

Through these interviews, I identified 12 main areas that people usually think about when deciding whether to have a child. I realized you don't have to think about every little "what if" question to make this decision and that trying to think of every scenario wasn't very helpful.

Then as I was researching and writing the book, and after being married for 13 years, I got pregnant. I had not yet made my definite "Yes" or "No" decision. My husband and I were at the point, "If it happens, I'm okay with it, and if it doesn't happen, I'm okay with it," which many books don't consider an option.

For the next few years, I took care of my son, learned how to be a mother, and kept working on the book. Having a child definitely changed my life and perspective of children. I started looking at the process of "How to Decide to Have a Child" differently. I asked myself, "Knowing what I know now—being a mom after struggling with the decision—what would help other people make a good decision for themselves, without wasting as much time as I did?" I felt I knew both perspectives. I realized that the things you think are important before you decide are not the things that are important after you have a child.

I also realized that making this type of decision doesn't just boil down to weighing the pros and cons and thinking rationally about the decision. Over the years, as more and more women have entered the rational-thinking workforce, we've started looking at decisions from this limiting perspective. After all, if many people did just consider the pros and cons of having a child, many more would not be having them. Having a child is a complex decision that combines our emotions, intuition, and spiritual beliefs, as well.

What you will get out of this book

I will give you an unbiased approach to your decision. I spent most of my life not wanting to have children and can relate to those people who are leaning in that direction. I also did have a child and understand firsthand what a wonderful experience it can be. I am not going to try to convince you one way or another. However, throughout this book, I will share the transformation that I experienced after having my child. There are books that rave about not having kids and justify why it works for the author, and there are books that rave about having kids and try to influence people to have more children. My main goal is that you will finish this book and be content and satisfied with whatever decision you make. This is YOUR decision, and YOU will make the best decision for YOU. That is my hope.

By reading this book, you will save a lot of time in making your decision, so you can spend more time living your life. There is so much information available about having children from a variety of disparate sources that it can be overwhelming to try to find and sort through it all. I know this firsthand as it took me a long time to hash through all the issues and research to find answers to my questions. In retrospect, I wish I had spend more time living my life, instead of pondering the "what ifs." In this book, I have identified the main issues so that you won't get confused, distracted, or suffer from information overload. (Although I do share a lot of information.)

In order to save time and reduce confusion, I have created a structure for your decision-making process. This structure will give you a path or plan to follow so you will feel more organization and focused as you contemplate the many issues that you ponder when making such an important decision. Because I understand the need for considering many sides of the decision, the process includes addressing the question from a rational, emotional, intuitive, and spiritual perspective.

I also share much data and research. People I interviewed who were struggling with their decision explained that they wanted a resource that provided facts and studies that would help educate them in important areas so they could make a better decision. They explained that reading books about other people's feelings and emotions didn't help much. In this book you get data, research, interviews, and anecdotes I share from my personal journey.

The first part of the book lays the foundation for your decision. I explain how the biological and natural process of having a child has become a choice, meaning it has become an option, not necessarily a "given." I also explain how your brain makes decisions, so you understand your internal process and can be as certain as possible that you are being true to yourself. As you will learn when making a decision, the way your brain functions creates biases that can sometimes mislead you if you aren't aware of them. Next, I give you other options besides "yes" or "no," depending on your situation and stage in life, that can help you live your life and be free of uncertainty. To further minimize distraction, I explain how certain questions don't provide any insight and ask that you not spend any more time thinking about them. These questions focus on comparing your life to others and wondering if you are "selfish" for having for not having children.

The second part of this book focuses on you and your current thoughts, feelings, and position about motherhood. Here you will spend some time being introspective to gain clarity of your current position – are you leaning toward having a child or not having a child? I suggest a few written exercises so you understand why you are thinking about having a child at this point in your life, how your childhood and parenting roles may be influencing you, your thoughts about pregnancy and childbirth, what maternal instinct is and how it may be influencing your decision, and how external influences are affecting your decision.

In the third section of this book, I share the 12 main factors people usually consider when deciding whether to have a child and provide current information and research so that you can make the best decision for yourself. These factors are: Population concerns, finances, health and body, significant other, emotional readiness, how to care for a child, impact on work and career, childcare and education, relationships with others, benefits of having children, determining whether you are the childfree type, and regret for deciding either way. By focusing on and learning about these main factors, you won't be wasting a lot of time getting distracted by outlying information that isn't pertinent. At the end of each section, I provide a thought-provoking question to illicit a response from you to determine if that factor is important to you.

In the fourth part of this book, you make your decision. Here you digest all the information you have learned and discover how to tap into your intuition to make the best decision for yourself.

My idealistic ambitions

The main reason I wrote this book is to help people think through the issues of having a child before they make their decision to have one. I want to give people a process to help them think through the issues—whether they have already made their decision or are still pondering—so they can better understand themselves and gain clarity and certainty about their decision. In the past, women weren't given a choice, and many women and men just had children because "that's what people did," to the detriment of their children. There are so many people who write about how their mothers (and fathers) didn't seem happy, couldn't handle motherhood, or just didn't know how to mother—Dr. Laura Schlesinger, Gloria Steinem, Oprah Winfrey, Christine Crawford (of *Mommie Dearest*).

Personally, I didn't think my mother enjoyed being a mother, and it had a negative impact on me. I love my mother and always wanted her to be happy, but I thought she'd be happier without the duties and responsibilities of raising children. Because of my experience, I want women and men to really be honest with themselves about who they are and if they are capable of taking care of a child. I believe a child deserves to come into this world feeling wanted and loved. If a person is not able to take care of a child, by all means, please don't have them. Please consider what is good and fair for the child.

Every day in the news we hear about parents harming or killing their children. Raising children is not easy, and the quality of care a child receives can be drastically affected by extraneous stressful events happening in a parent's life—like the loss of a job, divorce, or trying to earn enough money to support a family. Also, people may not be emotionally ready to have a child or have the knowledge or experience in how to care for one. I would like children to feel wanted and loved when they are brought into this world. They don't ask to be born, although some people think otherwise (that children choose their parents). So, it is the parents' responsibility to make sure they can handle it.

Through this book, I also want to bring together two opposing groups that sometimes have strong feelings about one another. As I was interviewing people about children, there was a clear and distinct bias between the parents and non-parents toward one another. Some parents have a negative view toward childfree people, and childfree people can be antagonistic toward parents and children.

People who knew they wanted to be childfree or were leaning in that direction, believed that society was too family and child-centric and felt pressure to conform and have children. They felt somewhat excluded and left out, and had to constantly defend their choice to deviate from the norm. The parents and people who wanted children believed that society was anti-family and anti-child. They said they felt a need to constantly defend their decision to have children. By helping people go through the process of deciding whether or not to have children, I hope they can reach a conclusion that is good for them, but also with respect for those people who decide otherwise.

The world is more interconnected than in the past. It's important to understand how our decisions impact each other and how we interact with one another through our lifetimes. I hope that parents can see that childfree people may pick up the slack at work sometimes as they tend to family issues, and I hope that childfree people realize that parents are doing their best to raise good citizens – the people that may someday be the doctor that saves their life or safely flies the plane to their next vacation. I hope parents will learn that some of these childfree people are the excellent teachers that are helping their children learn, and I also hope the childfree people will understand that childhood is just a phase or human development. Children aren't always going to be noisy, bouncy, sticky, messy beings (although I've met plenty of adults like this, too). Kids turn into adults and are adults much longer than they are children. So, by going through this process, it is my wish that we can come to understand and respect each other's decisions so that we can live and work in a more peaceful and enlightened way.

The Baby Dilemma

FOUNDATIONS FOR MAKING A CONFIDENT DECISION

provides you with a better understanding of the decision-making process and helps you to understand your feelings with more certainty. Then, when you do arrive at your decision of whether or not to enter into parenthood, you will have the confidence and peace of mind to know that it is, indeed, the right decision for you.

1. HAVING A CHILD IS A CHOICE

"No one can instruct us how to best live our lives; we have to figure out for ourselves what brings us our greatest satisfaction and pleasure. When you define how you want to live, you get to the heart of your personal happiness...We don't owe anyone a piece of our life against our wishes. It is our right and responsibility to choose what is right for us."
-Alexandra Stoddard, *Things Good Mothers Know* p, 116-117.

Deciding to have a child is a relatively new phenomenon in regards to human reproductive history. It's no longer a given. Throughout the world, it's become commonplace to see that more and more people are having fewer children. Obviously, you are not alone in trying to understand your feelings about having children.

Many women in the United States may not realize that the freedoms we enjoy on a daily basis have only been around for a relatively short period of time. Most of these have only occurred in the past 90 years. Women obtained the right to vote in the 1920s, became more accepted in the work world in the 1940s during World War II, earned equal pay and the right to control their fertility in the 1960s, and were granted the right to apply for credit in their own name as recently as the 1970s.

I interviewed women who were born in earlier years and had children in the 1940s and 1950s, asking them, "How did you decide to have children?" Nearly all of them stated it wasn't a decision or choice to make. "It's just what you did. Everyone had kids." Even when I asked my mother, she said the same thing, "That's what we did back then." No one really thought about it. At that time, women didn't have as many options as they do today.

Years ago, women who decided not to have children were considered anomalies, because everyone had the assumption that's what women did—they had babies. When someone didn't have a child, people assumed there was something medically wrong with them—that they couldn't have children. Yet, there were still a few trailblazers, such as Mae West, Amelia Earhart, and Katherine Hepburn,

Of the women I interviewed, one who is now in her 90s and decided not to have children early on said that she lived through the depression and wanted more out of life. She was a pinup girl in World War II and was also one of the first women to graduate from the Chicago Institute of Technology with an engineering degree, where she engaged in time and motion studies. She then worked in the Playboy mansion in Chicago and dated Adlai Stevenson. She told me that one of the main reasons she didn't have children was that she enjoyed sex too much. What a trendsetter. She was involved in her nieces' and nephews' lives, and that was satisfying for her.

However, she was not the norm. The fact that she decided not to have children was a rarity at that time, indeed. Only recently have people had the freedom to openly decide whether or not to have a child. In May 1960, the U.S. Federal Drug Administration gave approval for a pill that had been marketed for "menstrual disorders" to be sold as the birth control pill. Within a year, there were one million American users; within five years, six million women were on the pill. Then in 1965, the United States Supreme Court overturned state laws that prevented married couples from using contraceptives. In 1972, the court extended the right to contraception to unmarried people. In addition, Canada decriminalized contraception in 1972.

Also, during this time, the women's movement was gaining steam. When Betty Friedan wrote *The Feminine Mystique* in

1963, she identified a simple, but profound, need in women: the need to do meaningful work. It is said that through her book, women came to understand why they were unhappy and suffering from "a problem that had no name." The book gave women validation for the jumble of conflicting emotions they had been experiencing about their traditional roles with children and family and the potential opportunities they were missing.

Considering how long humans have been on this earth, 46 years since the legalization of contraceptives is a relatively short period of time for people to learn how to determine whether or not to have children. Prior, it was considered to be more of a biological process—something that was expected, that just happened. No wonder it's not a comfortable or easy decision for us to make. It's not something we are used to thinking about. And, let's not forget, only the most recent generations of people have been born with this option, myself included.

It only makes sense that when someone has more opportunities and options, other paths will not be taken. For generations, women have been told that having children is what made them special, yet, that doesn't resonate with many women. No longer held captive to motherhood expectations, women are now free to pursue these other interests. When the first women to experience this freedom ventured forth boldly and bravely, there was a backlash against their former lives as mothers. And, now after having tasted and experienced those newfound freedoms and adjusting to them as more common and pervasive, motherhood is once again being addressed.

Since generations of women have been born with the option to pursue their interests and talents, there will probably be fewer children born. Not everyone will want or desire to have children, but those that do will be able to make that decision based on their own internal desires, instead of an external view placed on them by society.

That is the motivation for this book—to help women understand their personal motivations and desires so they can get clarification of whether motherhood is a path they truly want to take.

With the joint influences of birth control and having more options in how to live our lives, more women and men have the freedom to engage in other activities in the world than being parents. The ability for women to manage their biology has caused the decision to have a child to become one that requires more thought.

Women waiting to have children

Surveys show that women are waiting to have children or choosing not to have them at all. In the United States, the average age of women having their children went from 21.4 in 1970 to 25 in 2006. In other developed countries, women are 27 to 29 years old when they have their first child. In New Zealand, the country where women wait the longest to have children, the average age is almost 30 before they have their first child.[1]

The age is lower in the United States because we have more teenage pregnancies than other developed countries – about 400,000 a year in 2010[2]. Although the number of teenage pregnancies is the lowest it's ever been, and has dropped 37% over two decades, it is still higher than other developed countries.[3] If fewer teens in the United States had children, the U.S. age for first time birth would be higher – around 28 to 29. In 2006, 21% of first births in the U.S. were to teenagers.[4]

The average age at first birth increased for all racial and ethnic groups in the United States between 1990 and 2006. The oldest average age at first birth was 28.5 years for Asian or Pacific Islander women, while the youngest was 21.9 years for Alaska Native women. The average age at first birth was 26 years for white women, 22.7 years for black women, and 23.1 years for Hispanic women.[5]

In addition, older mothers are becoming more prevalent. In 1970, one in 100 births was among women ages 35 and older, compared with one in 12 in 2006.[6] Between 2007 and 2008, women between 40 and 44 years of age actually had more babies during that period than they had in decades. [7]

The reasons people are waiting longer to have children include the pursuit of education and personal interests, or focusing on first becoming financially established. Plus, people are living longer, which means that they can start families later and still be able to take care of them. The people that I spoke with understood the sacrifices that having and raising a child requires and wanted to pursue their interests first. They felt that by taking care of their needs and getting established before they started a family, they would have more stability and be better parents.

Women having fewer children

In 1909, there were 30 births for every 1,000 people in the United States. Over the years, that has declined to 13.5 children per 1,000 people in 2009.[8] The most recent data shows that the fertility rate in the United States is 2.01 children per women.[9] Fewer families are having more than two children, and almost 75% of births in 2009 were first or second births. [10] And, this trend of fewer children is not just occurring in the United States. Developed countries throughout the world are experiencing declining fertility rates and populations. More

about this trend will be discussed in the Population Chapter in STEP 2: THE TOP 12 FACTORS TO CONSIDER.

More women deciding not to have children

During the last 30 years, the number of people not having children in the United States has risen to an all-time high. In June 2010, 1 in 5 women never had children, an increase from the 1970s when 1 in 10 women didn't.[11] Other statistics show that in 2008, 1.9 million women aged 40 to 44 (or 18%) were childless, compared to 1976, when only 580,000 women in that age group (or 10%) never gave birth. In 2006, 20% of U.S. women over the age of 40 did not have children,[12] and studies show that in 2002, about 22% of men 40 to 44-years-old had not fathered any children.[13] Childlessness has increased across racial and ethnic groups and among the higher education levels. White women remain the most likely not to have had a child, but the childless rates have grown more quickly for blacks, Hispanics, and Asians over the past decade.

Because of the years of school required for advanced education, the most educated women are still among those most likely to never give birth. In *Creating a Life: Professional Women and the Quest of Children*, Sylvia Ann Hewlett, mother of 5, surveyed 1,658 high achieving women – 40% were still childless at age 45.

One of the reasons women are not having children is the pattern of delaying marriage and having kids. Waiting too long, people delay until they can't have a child. This category of women and men who wait too long to have children has actually been categorized and called "Postponers." People are also freer and want to enjoy their lives and pursue their own interests. Having a child has become an option in life, instead of a given. There is also a drop in societal pressure to be a parent, along with career opportunities and improvements in birth

control options and effectiveness. Some working women who have risen up the corporate ladder and have higher incomes realize they can't or don't want to do it all.

Today, there are also more role models who delay or choose not to have children. In earlier years, childfree people were anomalies. Now they are prevalent and acceptable. Oprah Winfrey, George Clooney, Condoleezza Rice, Bill Mahre, Ellen DeGeneres, Jennifer Aniston, Cameron Diaz, Lauren Hutton, Betty White, Kevin Spacey, Diane Sawyer, Ayn Rand, Julia Child, Helen Mirren, Jay Leno, and Mother Theresa are just a few well-known celebrities who don't or didn't have children.

More options, more choices, more confusion

In today's world, we have so many more options and choices in how we want to live our lives. It is a freedom we are fortunate to have, living in a developed country. Yet, having so many choices and options can overwhelm and cause confusion, leading us to the point that we make no choice at all, thus impairing our well-being.

In *The Paradox of Choice: Why More is Less*, Barry Schwartz, a psychology professor at Swarthmore College, challenges the belief of many Western industrialized societies that claim having more choices increases our freedom and thus improves our overall welfare. He shows that too many choices can be counter-productive and become a source of pain, regret, worry about missed opportunities, and unrealistically high expectations. Dr. Schwartz asserts that having more choices actually has a negative effect on us and causes us to feel miserable about the decisions we make.

Dr. Schwartz claims that having more choices produces paralysis, instead of liberation. Too many options make it difficult for people to choose at all. They fear and anticipate

regret. When people do overcome their paralysis and make a decision, they are less satisfied with the result of that decision because they are always wondering about the option they didn't choose.

In his book, Dr. Schwartz shares results of a study that looked at workers' participation in their company's 401(k) program. When there were too many investment funds to choose from, the workers did not participate, even if their company matched their contributions. Once the number of fund options was reduced, people started to participate.

Other academics have shown similar results in their research. A study conducted in the United States and Europe by social psychologists showed that too many choices made decision making too difficult. A group of shoppers was given a choice of 30 jams to taste, and the researchers watched to see how too many choices affected the purchase of a particular brand of jam. There was no change in the amount of jam purchased. Two weeks later, the testing was redone, and shoppers were given only six jams to taste. This time, there was a 15% increase in the jam purchased. [14]

How does this research help us understand our own decision-making process? Because knowing that too many options causes confusion may help us understand why we hesitate and become more cautious when making a decision as important as having a child. We realize that some of apprehension and reluctance to make a decision stems from the fact that we have a multitude of choices in how we want to live our lives. We may be more cautious when making the decision because we fear that choosing one option may make us regret not choosing another, which can cause regrets.

For me, too many options was definitely a problem. There were so many things I wanted to see and do in life that I had a hard time narrowing it down. And, because I was more focused

on pursuing those interests, I didn't really start thinking about having a child until I was 32-years-old and already 6 years married.

Amanda, a 20-year-old college sophomore, explained to me that she's not even thinking of having a child at this point in her life. "When I started school, I was pre-med. Now after taking more advance chemistry and biology classes, I'm not sure. There are so many classes and majors that sound much more appealing to me. I want to use my college years to explore other areas that I didn't even consider when I was in high school. I'll think about having a child in the future. But, it's only one option. There's more world to explore than I ever realized."

Daniel, a 28-year-old college graduate who is travelling across Europe, told me that having a family and a child isn't a given anymore. "I don't know if I want a family. I'm in a confused state of life right now. I went to college and got my degree in accounting, passed the CPA exam, was lucky to get a job in a big accounting firm and then, after a few years, realized I don't want to be in a cube my entire life. I'm only going to be young once, and I want to take some time now and see the world. Plus, the job market stinks, and I'm not sure if I even want to be an accountant. There are so many options that I'm not sure where to focus." He told me he was taking time off so he can better focus out his next steps.

Christina, a 36-year-old mother of two children, told me that deciding whether to have a child wasn't clear for her until she turned 30. She said there were too many things she wanted to do. "I played a variety of sports in high school, went to college, earned a dual major in Political Science and Economics, and played golf on my college team. I then got an MBA, but also wanted to explore improv comedy. So, while getting my MBA, I participated in an improv program, which led me to a few roles

in some TV shows. But, then I met a guy – another actor—that made me think about marriage and having kids. It's not what I would say I planned. One thing led to another in a disorganized way. Now, I have two kids – two and four. And, I'm going to do try to do some freelance writing."

Although in this section I stress that having a child is more of a choice today, more than ever before, I wouldn't be providing you with a fair overview of your decision-making possibilities without mentioning the fact that almost half of the pregnancies in the United States are unplanned. According to the Alan Guttmacher Institute, which studies reproductive trends, 49% of pregnancies were unintended in 1994. Between 1987 and 1994, the rate of unintended pregnancies did drop by 16%,[15] but even recent data show that at least half of American women will experience an unintended pregnancy by age 45.[16]

Nonetheless, people have more opportunities to pursue and create the life they want. As a result, fewer people are having children. So, then, how do you know if having a child is a path you'd want to take? The next sections will give you an overview of how your brain works when making decisions and provide a framework for you to determine whether you want to have the experience of having a child in your life.

2. HOW OUR BRAINS WORK WHEN MAKING DECISIONS

Our lives are shaped and defined by the decisions we make. Some decisions are easier to make than others. Actions that we take every day, like what to eat for breakfast or what clothes to wear, aren't difficult because we've had many years of practice doing these things. However, there are some decisions that we just don't know how to process or approach. These decisions may be difficult because they are so complex; there are many personal variables, external variables, and unknowns. We become distracted because this question lingers on our minds, or we get stuck in life because we don't know how to approach the decision. If we could just figure out which direction to take, we could move forward.

Having a child is one of the most important decisions that a person can make. Other important decisions, such as whom to marry, where to go to school, or which profession to pursue, are all correctable or changeable after the fact. However, once you are a parent, you will always be a parent, even when your child is 45-years-old.

So how do you approach such a life-altering decision? Most would say that such a weighty decision should involve a lot of research and analysis to determine the best outcome for an individual. However, according to brain research, that is not the case. And, research has shown that your emotions and visceral reactions tend to influence your decisions more than you realize.

In this section, we'll explore some aspects of decision making, including:

1. Your decision will not be a completely rational decision, and you don't want it to be. Including your

emotions and instincts will help you a make a better decision.

2. Don't over think your decision. You can make a better decision by NOT over analyzing.

3. Your brain can only consider a certain number of factors when making a decision. That is why I provide you with the top 12 factors that people consider, and only certain ones will be important to you. Take your time when reading this book. Give your brain time to digest the information.

4. Be careful not to talk yourself into a decision. Sometimes your rational brain can override your emotional brain, even when your emotional brain knows what is best. Be aware of how your brain works so you can make the best decision for you.

5. Remember that we all have cognitive biases when we make decisions. We tend to want to avoid loss and may focus on the negative. These are only natural, but by understanding them, they won't lead you astray.

It's impossible to make a completely rational decision

Because having a child is a life-changing event, many people assume the best decision is made rationally by thinking through the pros and cons and determining what is in their best interest. It has been assumed that the ability to analyze facts—to overcome our feelings, instincts, and impulses—is the defining element of human nature. In the past, people thought reason and emotion were two separate parts of decision making and that reason should rein over impulsive emotions. Even today, reason is viewed as civilized, and emotions are crude and primitive.

In *How We Decide*, Jonah Lehrer explains how human brains make decisions and that there is no such thing as a completely rational self. MRI technology has shown that it's impossible for a brain to make a decision based only on reason. During MRI's, people's brain activity reveals how the emotional and rational parts of the brain work simultaneously to reach a conclusion.

"The mind is composed of different areas, many of which are involved with the production of emotion. Whenever someone makes a decision, the brain is awash in feeling, driven by its inexplicable passions. Even when a person tries to be reasonable and restrained, these emotional impulses secretly influence judgment."[1]

This doesn't mean that because our emotional brain is influencing us that we will automatically make good decisions. There are no universal solutions to decision making. Sometimes our feelings can lead us astray, and sometimes too much rational thought can get us stuck. In order to make good decisions, we need to use both parts of our brains. We need to learn when to listen to our emotions and/or reason through our options and carefully analyze the possibilities. We also have to come to terms with that reality that we may not feel 100% certain when we make our decisions, yet make them anyway. The secret, according to Lehrer, is to be aware of how you think and know when to use the different styles of thought.

Even though we are defined by our decisions, we are often unaware of what's happening inside our heads during the decision-making process. Here's a brief explanation of the pertinent parts. The limbic brain is often referred to as the emotional brain or primitive brain. It consists of several structures that are involved with memory and emotion and generate our "feeling response." The prefrontal cortex is the "rational" part of the brain and integrates these visceral emotions into the decision-making process. Most of what occurs in the brain as we make decisions are an interplay between many regions of the brain and take place almost instantaneously. Depending on the type of decision or problem we are facing, we may use one part more than the other.

Much of what we think is driven by our emotions. We develop these emotional reactions and learn to trust our instincts when we are doing something or being exposed to situations for a long enough period of time that they seem natural. In this instance, we aren't even aware that we are having an emotional response.

Lehrer explains how this happens. "The spindle neuron cells are able to convey emotions across the entire brain. Every time a person makes a mistake or encounters something new, the brain cells are busy changing themselves. After a while, they know what to expect. Neurons are continually incorporating the new information, turning a negative feeling into a teachable moment. Every time a person experiences a feeling of joy or disappointment, fear or happiness, their neurons are busy rewiring themselves, constructing a theory of what sensory cues preceded the emotions. The lesson is then committed to memory. Every emotion is really a summary of data, a visceral response to all the information that can't be accessed directly. The unconscious processes all types of data. It then translates the data into vivid emotional signals that were detected by the prefrontal cortex. You then act upon these subliminal calculations."[2]

The prefrontal cortex is an area associated with rational planning. It is this region that encourages a person to be patient, to second guess, and to act with more caution. When parts of our brain influence us to want things right away, our frontal cortex tells us to slow down and act with more self-control.

The emotional brain constantly sends out visceral signals about its likes and dislikes. The prefrontal cortex is like the director, monitoring the emotional reactions and deciding which to take seriously. The rational brain can't silence emotions, but helps to figure out which ones should be followed. The prefrontal cortex can transcend our impulses and figure out which feelings are useful and which ones should be ignored. If the emotional brain is pointing you in the direction of a bad decision, you can choose to rely on your rational brain instead. Prefrontal cortex exercises authority over its own decision-making process. The prefrontal cortex is linked to all parts of the brain. The prefrontal cortex allows a person to analyze any type of problem from every possible angle.

One thing to note is that the primitive/emotional brain is first to mature in a child, and the prefrontal cortex matures much later. Some brain research indicates that brain development is not complete until near the age of 25, which usually refers to the prefrontal cortex.[3] Because the prefrontal cortex is the last brain area to fully mature, scientists claim that this delayed developmental process explains the behavior of adolescents who are more likely than adults to engage in risky, impulsive behavior. According to some experts, teens make bad decisions because their brains aren't fully developed yet.

Thinking too much can lead to an erroneous judgment

Just because we have a prefrontal cortex to help us reason, that doesn't mean it has all the answers. It is possible to think too much. The prefrontal cortex and its reasoning ability is a powerful tool. Studies have shown that when the rational brain takes over the mind, people tend to make all sorts of decision-

making mistakes. They ignore the wisdom of their emotions and start looking for things they can't explain. Instead of going with the option that feels the best, a person goes with the option that sounds the best, even if it's not a good idea.

One famous study that supports this was conducted by Timothy Wilson, a psychologist at University of Virginia. He had his students simulate a jam taste test that *Consumer Reports* conducted. *Consumer Reports* had taste sensory experts sample and rank several types of jams based on sixteen different criteria. Wilson selected a few of the jams from the top, middle, and bottom rankings. The students performed almost as well as the experts and agreed as to which were the top and bottom jams. This experiment showed how brains are able to automatically pick out products that provide us with the most pleasure.

Wilson repeated the experiment. This time, he asked different college students to explain why they preferred one brand over another. The students were asked to fill out a questionnaire that forced them to analyze their first impressions and to consciously explain their impulsive preferences. This extra analysis influenced their judgment. These students actually preferred the worst jam as the best.[4]

This experiment has been cited on numerous occasions, illuminating the danger of always relying on the rational brain. This and similar tests show that, in certain situations, our gut instinct, rather than rational thought, really knows what is best for us. There is such a thing as over analysis. When people are tasked to think about their preferences, their thoughts override their instincts. Thinking too much about something causes us to focus on variables that don't actually matter. When we over think at the wrong moment, we cut ourselves off from the wisdom of our emotions, which are much better at

assessing actual preferences. Thus, we lose the ability to know what we really want.

Wilson conducted another experiment. He asked female college students to select their favorite poster. Their choices were classical Monet and van Gogh paintings and humorous cat posters. Before making their choices, the subjects were divided into two groups. The first group was instructed to simply rate each poster on a scale from 1to 9. The second group had to fill out a questionnaire that asked them why they liked or disliked each of the five posters before they selected the one they liked best. At the end of the experiment, each of the subjects took her favorite poster home. Two weeks later, they would be asked about their decisions.

The two groups made very different choices. Ninety-five percent of the non-thinkers chose either the Monet or the van Gogh. They instinctively preferred the fine art. However, those subjects that thought about their poster decisions first were almost equally split between the paintings and the humorous cat posters.

When Wilson followed up with the women a few weeks later to see which group had made the better decision, the members of the non-thinking group were much more satisfied with their choice of posters, while 75% of the people who chose the cat posters regretted their selections. Nobody regretted the artistic posters. The women who listened to their emotions ended up making much better decisions than the women who relied on their reasoning powers. The more people thought about which posters they wanted, the more misleading their thoughts became. Self-analysis resulted in less self-awareness.

Our brains can get overwhelmed with too much data

When deciding whether to have children, we can get overwhelmed with the high amount of information there is to consider. We live in a society where we are inundated with information everywhere we go. Studies have shown that our prefrontal cortex can get intimidated by all that data. The conscious brain can only handle about seven pieces of data at any one moment.[5] Others claim the brain can hold only six to ten pieces of data when making a decision. More than that, and the brain becomes overwhelmed.

Ap Dijksterhuis, a psychologist at the University of Amsterdam, conducted an experiment where he asked subjects to select the "best" of four cars. Each car had 4 (simple) or 12 (complex) attributes. These attributes were either positive or negative. After reading information about the cars, the subjects were split into two groups. One group was asked to think about the cars for a period of time and choose their favorite one; the other group was distracted for the same period of time, then asked to choose their favorite car. The thinkers made better choices with fewer attributes, but performed poorly under complex circumstances. However, the distracted group—those that had to choose based on their emotions—did well and selected the best car under both the simple and complex circumstances.[6]

This test showed that when making a decision, too many variables can confuse the prefrontal cortex. Instead, it will tend to fix on one variable that may or may not be relevant. The rational brain tries to oversimplify the situation. The longer people spend analyzing their options, the less satisfied they are with their decisions. Their rational faculties had been overwhelmed by the choices and options they had.

Be cautious of talking yourself into a wrong decision

Be careful about talking yourself into the wrong choice when your rational brain overrides your emotional brain. Your expectations can influence your experience and your decisions.

One test done at Stanford University showed that the rational prefrontal cortex can erroneously override our emotional instincts when considering information the cortex finds exciting or interesting. In this experiment, the frontal cortex was excited by the "price" or "cost" of an item. Here, people were given five wines to taste. The wines were identified by price: $5, $45 and $90. However, during the tasting, the same wine was re-tasted with a different price without the subjects' knowledge. Each wine was sipped by each person while inside an MRI machine. People consistently reported that the more expensive wine tasted better, even though the same wine was also tasted at a lower price.

The MRIs showed that the prefrontal cortex responded to the price of wine, rather than the wine itself. The more expensive wines made the frontal cortex more excited. This brain region made the people think that the wine was better due to its high price. Even when the test was conducted with the Stanford University wine club, the members were also misled by the high price.

The scientists then gave the people the wine samples in a blind tasting – with no prices revealed. In this instance, people reversed their previous choices and gave the cheapest wine higher scores.

Be aware of your decision-making biases so they don't lead you astray

Decision-making biases are errors or inaccurate beliefs that may mislead us into making a decision that isn't the best for us. One way to reduce their effect on our decisions is to be aware of them. I mention them in the context of deciding whether or not to have a child to help you understand how they can possibly influence your decision.

Loss Aversion is a bias that causes us to avoid anything that seems like a loss. People tend to exhibit a greater sensitivity to losses than to equivalent gains. We are wired to dislike potential losses. This bias will cause you to avoid a loss, rather than going for what you want. People will avoid investments, jobs, or relationships if they feel they will have something to lose, especially money. Losing $100 hurts more than the pleasure of winning $100. There were many people I interviewed who said they didn't want to have children because they were too expensive, and they would rather spend their money on something else. Many of them said they would lose their freedom and ability to travel.

Inertia bias is when you procrastinate to make a decision because you feel trapped in your circumstances and don't know how to change. Each option has advantages and disadvantages, and that conflict causes you to postpone the decision and seek additional information. You may feel stuck. In order to overcome this bias, it's best to put a voluntary constraint on yourself by giving yourself a deadline.

I can relate to this bias. I thought if I could interview one more person or read one more book, I would then be able to make a decision. I also tried to put a time limit on myself, saying I wanted to make a decision by the time I turned 40.

24

Selection bias consists of our attitudes, interests, experiences, and background that cause us to selectively see what we want to see. Our age, gender, race, early childhood, experiences, occupation, and family status are other examples. Couples with children see the world very differently than perceived by childfree couples. We selectively organize and interpret events based on our biased perceptions and then call this interpretation reality. I encountered this bias when I interviewed people *with children* who told me that they felt that society was *not child-friendly*, and then when I spoke to *childfree* people who told me that society is *too child-friendly and family-centric* and they felt left out. We can minimize these biases by increasing our awareness or by confronting our expectations and consider how we might be misinterpreting the situation.

Confirmation bias is when your reasoning consists of finding arguments to support what you already believe. People don't want to hear information that causes them to question their beliefs, and they ignore the information they don't want to hear. To overcome this bias, it's good to start by being honest about your motives. Are you still deciding whether or not you want to have a child, or are you really looking for information and ways to confirm what you already believe? In order to make a good decision for yourself, it's better to approach your decision with an open mind, where you are open to all possibilities.

Representative bias causes you to assess the likelihood of an event based on how closely it resembles some other event or set of events. To overcome this bias, it's best to remember that what happened in the past has no impact on what occurs in the future. For example, you may have watched your parents' struggle when raising you, and you feel that it would be the same for you. However, this isn't the case. Your experience can be very different.

Negativity bias is when bad is stronger than the good. We naturally focus and remember the negative, rather than the positive. The negative factor is something that may be dangerous to us, so the memory of it tends to be stronger. It also takes more positive experiences to override a negative one. It has been said that five positive comments are needed to override one negative comment. When thinking about having children, that may explain why people are at a loss when asked about good reasons to have kids and why they can list more reasons not to.

3. YOUR OPTIONS

When I've talked to people about deciding whether or not to have children, one issue that comes up is why people feel forced to make a "yes" or "no" decision. Eventually, of course, everyone will make a decision to have children or not have children in their lifetime. But, at what point does it have to be made? And, why does it feel like no one can change their mind? Of course, the reality is that up until you do have children, you are always free to change your mind.

Although a yes or no decision would be ideal, as our society and lives have become more complex, a "yes" or "no" answer may not be suitable for your situation. Yet, I know firsthand that it is better to reach some kind of determination so you can free up your mind and energy. Not coming to some kind of determination can make you feel stuck or like you are living in limbo. That is why I have come up with other options for you to consider. Flexible options will give you the freedom to live your life until your life dictates a definitive choice.

It's okay to change your mind

Going through law school and business school, I was exposed to different theories of leadership. Many of these theories seemed to emphasize that a good leader needed to have the quality of decisiveness—the ability to make a decision and stick with it. Indecisiveness or changing one's mind was frowned upon. Those people who can't decide are "flipfloppers." We assume that when someone changes their mind that they can't make decisions, when it might be they are altering their plan because the situation has changed or new information was learned. When it comes to something as important and irreversible as having a child, you have the right to change your mind until you have a child or can't physically have them. I've seen people change their minds through the years, and they are very successful and happy people.

Sandra was a 25-year-old CPA when I met her 20 years ago. She said the immediate family she grew up in wasn't emotionally supportive, and she really couldn't wait to leave for college. Throughout most of her life, she didn't want to have children, but she did marry a boyfriend she met at her university. However, when her grandmother, the only family member with whom she did have a close relationship, died she said she just knew she wanted to have children. She said losing this close relationship made her realize that family was important to her. She said that her grandmother's death woke her up to the finite quality of life, and helped her understand how much she valued human relationship and connection. She said she didn't know what that quality was until it was gone. There was a love that she wanted to bring into the world and foster, and that was love for another human being. She went on to have three children.

Sometimes your decision is based on your situation

Many of our life experiences aren't black and white. As our lives progress, we are exposed to different people and new situations, which can inspire us to want children or not. If you don't already know that you want to have a child, you may feel differently in the "right" situation—meaning the "right" situation for you—not that there is a right situation for wanting a child. If you are currently not in a relationship, but meet someone a few years later, it may feel right to have a child with that person. But you could also meet someone who doesn't want to have children, and you are happy with that, as well.

For example, Amanda was 33 years old when she met Greg, who was about 15 years older. They married, and during the first three years of their marriage, they talked about having kids. Greg's first wife had died of cancer, and he never had children. He said he always wanted them, but didn't with his first wife. Amanda loved Greg very much and thought he'd make a great father. He was loving, kind, nurturing, patient, and fun. She said they also were financially secure and had loving family living close by who would be happy if they had children and would help out. They were both open to making this happen. But, as they were discussing having a child, Greg learned he had cancer. Within a few years, he passed away.

After a few years of mourning, Amanda started dating again at the age of 41. This time, she met Daniel who was about 20 years older than herself and had three children from previous marriages. He was a wonderful, loving, and fun man. He had also had a vasectomy. When they were talking about getting married, Daniel said he'd have his vasectomy reversed if she really wanted to have children. He didn't want to prevent her from having the chance to have children.

Amanda shared with me that her decision not to have children was very situational. With Greg, she felt it was a good situation to have children, until he got cancer. Daniel already had children, he and she were older, and she was just in a different place in life. Amanda also was very involved in helping raise her younger brother and nephew and likes to visit her nieces and nephews. She said she doesn't feel that she is missing anything.

We can't always predict the way our lives will go

Some people claim that it's better to have a definite plan and goal in life—that by knowing what you want, you will then live your life to make it happen. So if you decide that you want to have children, you will start living your life to make that happen.

Although that is probably great advice for some people and situations, I have met and interviewed many women who I know who would like to have children, but are still looking for the right person. Deciding that you want to have children doesn't necessarily mean it will happen.

Joanna, a marketing professor at a state college, always knew she wanted to have children. Yet, at the age of 49, she hasn't met anyone and knows she doesn't want to have a child on her own. She said it took her three months to mourn the loss of her "ideal" life and get on with living the one she has. She said she gets a lot of fulfillment teaching and from spending time with her friends' children. Although she was sad for awhile, she's content now.

Another couple, who both wanted children desperately until the wife's infertility proved too difficult to remedy, decided to adopt. Steve, the husband, said his father died when he was younger and he always had wanted a family. Valerie, the wife, said she'd wanted to have children since she was a little girl, and became a pediatric nurse because of it. This couple oozed and dripped loving family energy. I almost wished they would adopt me. So after three years of infertility treatments, they decided to adopt. Two months after their adopted baby boy came home to them, Valerie discovered she was pregnant.

More alternatives in making your decision

Another reason I think that people need more alternatives than just "yes" or "no" is that people may get pressured into a decision in order to avoid constant scrutiny of their situation. June, a child therapist, is 38, and her boyfriend, a finance manager, is 34. They have been living together for a few years. At this time, they don't want to have children. But, June says in a few years she may. She's still not sure. Friends and family keep asking them questions about whether they are going to have children. June says that although she's not decided, she's getting to the point of responding, "No, we don't want to have children," in order to get people to stop the prying and questioning. But, she's afraid to tell people "No" and then turn up pregnant two years from now. She said, "Then everyone will think we were irresponsible or that our baby wasn't wanted."

Here are decision-making answers and responses that you may reach as you go through life and grow and change as a person. Remember, the purpose of these options is to help you reach some type of decision and give you a level of "closure" so that you can move forward in life, without constantly thinking about or over-analyzing your situation. And, remember, you are always free to change your mind, until you actually have a child.

Some of your options

1. "Yes."
2. "No."
3. "I'm waiting to decide until..." Use this option when you aren't quite sure how you feel about wanting to have children or not, but have a goal or milestone to meet. "I'm waiting until I graduate from college to think about it." Or "I will wait until I'm at least 25-years-old to decide."
4. "I may want children if I'm with the right person." This response is good if you know that you would only want to have children while in a relationship with the "right" person.
5. "We are enjoying our relationship right now and want to see how it develops before we decide." Sometimes a relationship goes through its own evolution before the partners decide they want to have a child. We are not

all static individuals. We do grow and change over time, depending on our environment and the life events that we experience.

6. "We have thought about it, and we are willing to let fate decide." Or "If it happens, it happens." Couples have discussed whether or not they want to have a child and get to the point that if they have a child, they will be fine with it, and if they don't, they will be fine with it.

7. "I'm open to seeing what life brings." I've interviewed people who were very flexible in their approach and didn't feel they had to make a decision one way or the other. They said they would see what life presented to them.

8. You are also free to create your own option, as well, and tailor it to your situation. There is no right or wrong when deciding whether to have a child.

4. DISTRACTING THOUGHTS

As I was interviewing people, recurring questions and comments kept coming up. People got caught up in what other people were experiencing and whether or not they were selfish in their decision making. But, these questions and comments don't help people make their decision to have a child or help them move forward in making their decision. In fact, this type of thinking can very often mislead an individual into not making the best decision for themselves.

1. Focusing on other people and their experiences

During my interviews, I heard similar comments:

"I don't want to have kids because everyone I know with kids is unhappy."

"I don't want to have kids because people with kids don't look like they are having fun."

"I want to have kids because I see what a special relationship that mom has with her kids."

"I want to have children because I see how much fun that family has."

As humans, we are constantly observing our environment and making assessments. We are looking out for dangerous situations so we can protect ourselves. At the same time, we are looking for pleasurable situations so that we can pursue happiness. Yet, as much as we like to think we can, we cannot gauge someone else's happiness. In fact, we even have a hard time explaining our own feelings of happiness. Looking at other's experiences and trying to predict our own in a similar situation doesn't work.

In *Stumbling on Happiness*, Daniel Gilbert explains that happiness is a subjective experience that is difficult to describe to ourselves and to others. Even evaluating people's claims as to their own happiness is tricky. [1]

In his book, Gilbert explains how our experiences are unique unto us, and no one can really know what that is like. He cites a study that examined the happiness of conjoined twin sisters, women who have been joined at the forehead since birth. Both are "joyful, playful and optimistic." When asked if they wanted to undergo surgical separation, they said, "No." Many people think that you really couldn't be happy in such a situation. Yet, these twins say they like being together, and research shows that communicating conjoined twins want to stay together.

In a speech Gilbert gave at a TED conference, he explains that our prefrontal cortex acts as an experience simulator. It allows us to have an experience in our head before we try it out in real life. Yet, it's not accurate. In his speech, he asked the audience to use their experience simulator and determine which reality they would rather choose: winning a $314 million lottery or becoming a quadriplegic. He says that most of us would probably pick the lottery winner. However, he shares the data on how happy these two groups of people are. He says that after a year of losing their legs and after a year of winning the lottery, "lottery winners and paraplegics are equally happy with their lives."[2]

Trying to gage the happiness of others in order to make your decision may not be a good idea. This applies to both the people who think people who have children are miserable and those people who think childfree people must be miserable because they don't have kids. And, the research shows that when we try to assess whether we will be happy in a future situation, we aren't accurate. The only way you are going to know what it is like to have a child is to have a child. The bottom line is, don't waste your time looking at what other people are doing or experiencing since you probably can't accurately assess their level of happiness. The experience of having a child or not having a child is going to be unique unto you.

2. "I'm selfish" if I have or don't have kids

The reason why I am advising you not to waste your time thinking about whether or not you are selfish to have or not have children is because it won't help you make a decision. First, both groups of people—those who have children and those who don't have children—told me they thought they were labeled selfish for having or not having children. So, if this is the case, it seems that no matter what you decide, someone may label you as selfish. One couple in their 30s who decided not to have children said people thought they were selfish because they could spend their money on restaurants, vacations, cars, and other items they valued. Other people who had children said that people thought they were selfish for having kids because the world already has enough people and that having children just contributed to overpopulation and the ensuing environmental deterioration. People with children also said their co-workers probably thought they were selfish because their childcare commitments sometimes required them to leave work early or miss work.

Second, I believe that deciding to have a child is an inherently selfish decision. And I don't think there is anything wrong with that. I know some people have sensitivities with regard to the word "selfish," and just hearing that word causes some to become defensive. To make sure we understand one another, I am using the definition of "selfish" defined by the World English Dictionary as "chiefly concerned with one's own interest and advantage, especially to the total exclusion of the interests of others."

For those who think that being selfish when deciding to have a child is somehow wrong or harsh, let me explain. Being selfish when making a decision does not make you a selfish person. Being selfish when you make this decision is taking into consideration your interests, needs, desires, wants, aspirations, skills, talents, passions, and dreams. And, a person deciding whether to have a child will automatically consider their self-interest.

For example, if you are a person who loves children and wants to have the experience of caring for, nurturing, and raising a child, you will decide to have one because it is something you desire and want. In your thought process, there is probably a reason you use to explain your decision, and this will probably be beneficial to you. Such as, you may say that you want to care for a child, for the child's well-being. You may think that you are not getting anything out of it. But you are. You are getting a positive and emotional response for your altruistic actions. It has been shown in brain studies using MRI technology that our brains light up when we engage in doing nice things for other people, and that it make us feel good.

However, if you are a person who doesn't want children, your decision will also be based on your own interests, needs, desires, wants, aspirations, skills, talents, passions and dreams, as well. You know that you aren't interested in taking care of or raising children and may find other pursuits more appealing. There is nothing wrong with this. Not everyone has the same interests and desires. You are doing what's in your best interest. It probably wouldn't be a good idea or fair to a child if you weren't able to care or provide for it. So, no matter what you decide, you are probably making a selfish decision.

SUMMARY

Some things to keep in mind when deciding to have a child:

1. Deciding to have a child is a relatively new phenomenon in regard to human reproductive history. It's no longer a given. More and more people are having less children throughout the world. You are not alone in trying to understand your feelings about having children.

2. Your decision will not be a completely rational decision, and you don't want it to be. Including your emotions and instincts will help you a make a better decision.

3. Don't over think your decision. You can make a better decision by NOT over analyzing.

4. Your brain can only consider a certain number of factors when making a decision. That is why I provide the top 12 factors that people consider, and only certain ones will be important to you. Take your time when reading this book. Give your brain time to digest the information.

5. Be careful not to talk yourself into a decision. Sometimes your rational brain can override your emotional brain, even when your emotional brain knows what is best. Be aware of how your brain works so you can make the best decision for you.

6. Remember that we all have cognitive biases when we make decisions. We tend to want to avoid loss and may focus on the negative. These are only natural, but by understanding them, they won't lead you astray.

7. Remember, you don't necessarily have to make a "yes" or "no" decision. Understand your situation and what you need to do so that you can move forward, living your life.

8. Don't waste time thinking of other people's experiences –whether they are happy with or without children. You cannot possibly accurately assess their level of happiness and satisfaction with life. And, your experience will be completely unique to yourself, that no one else will probably be able to adequately assess.

9. Don't worry about being selfish in your decision. Making this decision should be a selfish decision, and no matter what you decide, it seems that people will think you are selfish anyway.

5. DECIDING TO HAVE A CHILD IN THREE STEPS

Now that we understand a little about how our brain works when making decisions, we are ready to move on to the decision-making process. This process is based on much of the brain research I shared in the earlier sections.

More specifically, I am applying the guidance of Ap Dijksterhuis, who advises the following when making complex decisions: "Use your conscious mind to acquire all the information you need for making a decision. But, don't try to analyze the information with your conscious mind. Instead, go on a vacation while your unconscious mind digests it. Whatever your intuition then tells you is almost certainly going to be the best choice."[1]

In summary, it's a three step approach:

Step 1. Start with YOU. In this step, you will get clear about your thoughts and feelings about motherhood and having children. You will examine:

- how your childhood may be influencing your thoughts about children
- whether you have tokophobia – the fear of pregnancy or giving birth
- whether or not you have maternal instinct, and if it is necessary before having a child,
- what is your current position in your decision-making process,
- examine other factors that may be influencing your decision.

At this point, you will write down your thoughts and experiences so you can get clear about your situation.

Step 2. THE 12 MAIN FACTORS. In this step, I share and explain THE 12 MAIN FACTORS people usually consider when deciding whether to have a child. I also provide factual information, research, and anecdotes from my interviews. At the end of each chapter, there will be questions to help you assess your position on each subject so you can identify those factors that really concern you.

Step 3. Making the decision. During this step, you integrate your thoughts from the previous sections and tap into your intuition to make the best decision for yourself.

Through the rest of the book, try to keep an open mind. If you feel you already know that you want or don't want to have children, I ask that you take a step back and try to approach the following material with no preconceived judgments. Much of the brain research shows that it's best to gather data from a wide variety of sources and be able to accept some ambiguity and uncertainty when in the decision-making process. If you already know your decision, your brain is more likely to focus on whatever facts are available to support your decision.

It has been said that a good decision-maker is more likely to study his own decision-making process and how he reaches his decision. Information you learn in the rest of this book may cause conflict and disagreement within different parts of your brain. Actively resist the urge to suppress the confusion or the arguments. Your brain will want to repress inner contradictions. Instead, try to be an observer and take the time to listen to what all the different parts of the brain areas have to say.

STEP ONE:

IT'S ALL ABOUT YOU

STEP 1 - IT'S ALL ABOUT YOU

In this first step, we take some time to understand what you think and feel about having a child and becoming a mother. I ask you to try to be as honest as you can with yourself. It's not always easy to be self-aware and know our inner motivations, and it's not always easy for us to articulate our innermost feelings.

When I first began wondering whether or not to have a child, I started reading book after book to try to find something that would trigger an "aha" moment in me, where I would just know, "Yes, I want a child" or "No, I don't want a child." But, I didn't find anything that struck me with such insight. The answer wasn't going to come from some outside inspiration, but from within myself. But, my insides were confused.

I did seek out a therapist to help me sort through my past so that I could better understand how I felt about having a child and motherhood. By taking the time to do this, I felt more comfortable that in moving forward in my life, I didn't have to let my past define my future.

I'm not a therapist, and my intention isn't to conduct therapy in this book. I simply want you to realize that our past experiences can impact how we think and feel about relationships, families, parenting, and children. In this section, we will spend a little time gaining clarity about your situation.

In the next sections, we'll examine:

1. **Why are you thinking about having a child now?**
    What is prompting you to think about having a child now? What has transpired in your life to make you think about being a mother?

2. **What was your childhood experience?** Do you come from a large family that loves children and you want to have them, too? Was your childhood so good that you want to also nurture another human being? Does it sound like a fulfilling experience? Or maybe you didn't have such a great childhood, but are still interested in having a child, but aren't quite certain.

3. **How do you feel about pregnancy and childbirth?** There are women who may be afraid of pregnancy and childbirth. Because of this, they think they don't want children. There are women who also want children but will avoid having them because of their fear.

4. **Do you have a maternal instinct?** One reason many women cite when saying they don't want children is that they don't have a maternal instinct. Many women are saying they don't feel nurturing toward children. Does that mean they shouldn't have children?

5. **Factors that could be influencing your decision.** This section explores factors that may be influencing your decision, such as your age, health, the relationship that you are in, your extended family, friends, religion, and personal values.

6. **Write it out.** This section helps summarize where you are in your thought process. The goal is to help you organize and structure some of your feelings and thoughts. Take the time to write down your answers to the questions.

1: Why Are You Thinking About Having a Child Now?

Ask yourself why you are making this decision now. What is going on in your life that made you think about having a child? Is this about a desire to have a child, or is there something that has happened that has made you think about having a child? See if there is something else going on in your life that may be prompting or influencing you. There is nothing wrong with having an external motivator. Below are some scenarios to help you start thinking about your own situation.

- You are in a relationship with a terrific person that you love and trust, and who makes you feel safe and secure. At dinner the other night, you just thought they'd be someone great to have a child with.

- You are 35-years-old and are having biological clock concerns. You realize that in "X" number of years you may not be able to a have a child, so you need and want to decide soon.

- You have always wanted a child, but are not sure if you are in a position to do it or if you can handle it at this point in your life.

- You are in a job you don't like and don't feel fulfilled in, and you wonder if having a child would be more fulfilling.

- You are in a relationship with someone who wants to have a child, but you aren't sure that this is what you want.

- Your relationship is not going well, and you think having a child will bring you together or provide a reason to stay together.
- You're not sure what else to do with your life and having a child would give you a purpose and identify in the world.
- You've gone to a friend's baby shower, and now you are wondering whether you'd like to have a child.
- Your friend just had a baby, and you are wondering if you would want one, too.
- You just read that another celebrity had a child, and it causes you to think of your situation.

Did something just happen in your life that is causing you to ponder life or mortality, like having a grandparent, parent, or other relative become ill or die? Robin was 28-years-old when her mother was diagnosed with cancer, and she wasn't dating anyone at the time. Her mother's diagnosis caused her to start thinking about having a family. "I felt an urgency because I felt that my mother may not be around, and I wanted my children to know her. It was strange, because I was pretty content with my life and not having children until then."

Or did you meet someone that made you think about having a child with them? A 38-year-old Ivy League Ph.D. said that when she was married to her first husband, she didn't want to have children. "I didn't want them at the time, and he wasn't really father material." Then she met her second husband and said that she wanted to have children with him. "The second time, I was older and wiser, and that was probably a factor, but my second husband just seemed more of the father type." She shared that her first husband did remarry and have children with someone else.

Sometimes our motivations may be unrealistic, impractical, or unethical. For example, are you thinking about having a child because you are unhappy in your current relationship and think it will make it better? A professional athlete and father told me that he and his wife were having marital problems, and after discussing it, they thought that having a child would make it better. They thought the love they would feel for a child and the caretaking of the child would bring them closer together. They ended up having a baby girl, who they did love. But, about two years later, they were divorced.

Are you trying to trap someone into a relationship? I am almost embarrassed that I am writing this because I would like to think that women are above this, but I know that it has happened. Having that child gives them a lifetime connection to the father, even if the relationship isn't good for either of them.

I had an adult woman tell me about how her mother misled her father. When her parents met, she told me, her father told her mother explicitly that he didn't want children because he had a child from a previous marriage. And, her mother agreed. However, after they got married, her mother intentionally got pregnant. After several years, the marriage dissolved, and the daughter says she has issues about it. She has a decent relationship with her father, but not her mother.

Did a sibling just have a child, and you feel left out or a bit envious of the attention? Or did a sibling have a child, and now you are questioning your decision to have one after seeing the realities of being a parent? A couple in their mid-twenties have been married for about two years and said they always wanted children and that they were going to start soon. But then the wife's brother had a child, and as they witnessed the realities of parenthood, they are now questioning their original thought

47

about having children. "Seeing my brother and how much his life changed was a wake-up call for us," the woman said. "I'm not sure if I really want that lifestyle anymore. We want to re-evaluate our position."

QUESTION:

Why do you think you are contemplating having children at this point in your life?

2: WHAT WAS YOUR CHILDHOOD EXPERIENCE?

When I read *Parenting From the Inside Out: How A Deeper Self-Understanding Can Help You Raise Children Who Thrive*, by Daniel Siegel and Mary Hartzell, the first sentence hit me, "How you make sense of your childhood experiences has a profound effect on how you parent your own children." Although I wasn't sure if I wanted to be a parent, I wanted to understand how my childhood could possibly influence the way I'd parent a child, if I did end up having one. I felt prompted to seek a therapist to gain more clarity about myself, how I was parented, my family dynamics, my relationship with family members, and how my childhood influenced the way I behave and thought. It was an invaluable experience that helped put my past in perspective so that my past wouldn't influence my decision-making or my future. I was free to create the life I wanted.

I will admit that at first I didn't want to "go there" – into my past. Mainly because, although I knew that my childhood wasn't perfect, I didn't want to admit to someone else that maybe I wasn't loved like I wanted and needed to be, and was hurt by it. It's not comfortable to put our parents on trial for how they treated us, since we all know they did the best they could.

I found when I interviewed people and asked about their childhood, some were fine with sharing that they went to therapy to understand their past, and others quickly cut me off. Some told me that their lives may not have been perfect, but they were fine with it and just wanted to live their lives. They didn't want to be "a case study like someone on a reality TV show," where people are "sniveling about their 'poor me' story." Some considered it a weakness to discuss their childhood.

Your childhood can directly influence our decision to have children

In Laura S. Scott's book, *Two is Enough: A Couple's Guide to Living Childless by Choice*, she conducted a survey of childless people to determine what motivated them to not have children. Almost 42% of childfree people selected the option: "I have seen or experienced firsthand the effects of bad or unintentional parenting, and I don't want to risk the chance that I might perpetuate the situation," as their primary reason for not wanting children.

I originally was one of those people who didn't want to waste a lot of time delving into my past. I didn't want to admit to myself that maybe I didn't have the best childhood or that my parents didn't seem happy. I wanted everything to be fine. However, the reality is that this was a major factor in why I didn't want to have children. I saw that my mother didn't seem happy with her family life or being my mother. I was never close to my father and really never had a relationship with him after they divorced when I was 13. I was told that children ruin your life, and I viewed having children as a chore and major obstacle to doing more "interesting" things in life. I had to go back into my past, so that I could put it in perspective in order to move forward on my own terms.

Examining your childhood doesn't mean you will decide not to have a child if you didn't have the best experience. You're only reviewing it to see how it may have influenced your perception of having children. It is just one factor to consider. Looking at the past will help you to live your life based on what you want in life, instead of the experience you were exposed to as a child. As adults, we are free to design and recreate the lives we want.

Examples of how childhood can affect our decision to have children

Brad, a 58-year-old Ivy League-educated district sales manager for a medical device company, told me he finally realized when he was 48-years-old that his childhood family life was probably a major factor in his decision not to want to marry and have children. He grew up with a volatile father who would throw dinner plates against the wall, and one Christmas, threw the decorated Christmas tree out the front door. He said his mother and older brother both died relatively young from alcohol abuse. He said he didn't feel like his father enjoyed being a father and didn't enjoy being with him as a child, and that he didn't know what it would take to be a father. He added that he really didn't want to learn, either. But, he repeatedly assured me throughout our interview that he wasn't a wounded, "poor-me" kind-of guy. He told me that his "hell" of a childhood wasn't the only factor in his decision. He said he liked his job and his life the way it was.

Laurie, a 40-year-old attorney in New Mexico, told me that her grandmother really raised her and her brothers because her mother was a drug addict. She said her childhood was very hard and caused her extreme pain, and she had to learn to be self-reliant and take care of her two younger brothers at a young age. Laurie said her only role model for mothering came from her grandparents, and although she thought they did the best they could, she still feels that she wouldn't know how to be a good mother. She is responsible, but not quite sure if she could handle taking care of a young child. She said she already felt a little like a mother since she helped raise her brothers and really doesn't think that she's ready to do it again.

Another couple in their early 30's said they both knew they wanted kids because they enjoyed their childhoods and that having children would allow them to relive some of those good times and share those similar kind of moments with their children. They wanted to share the joys of childhood and a family life they had experienced with their children. They both claimed they had decent, although not perfect, childhoods. They said their siblings would probably have a different perspective on their youth, since some of their siblings have decided not to have children.

A 28-year-old married graduate psychology student told me that she didn't feel she had a good childhood. Her father would work during the days, and her mother worked as a nurse at night. She was never close to her mother, who was always busy. She says she and her brother raised themselves. Yet, she did well in school and had a good relationship with her father. She went to college and met a guy who she ended up marrying. He came from a family that was very close. They enjoyed being with each other and actively fostered these relationships. She says, even with her childhood, she would love to have children with her husband, and he wants them, as well. She says she wants to be a stay-at-home mother while her children are younger.

What was your childhood like?

Take some time and answer the following questions:

- How would you describe your childhood – early years, teen years, adult years? Was it a positive or negative experience for you?
- What was your mother like, and what did you learn from her about being a parent?

- What was your father like, and what did you learn from him about being a parent?
- What was their relationship like? Were they happy? What did they teach you about being in a relationship?
- Did your parents ever express to you whether they liked being parents or not?
- Did your parents ever encourage you to have or not have children?

QUESTION:

How do you think your childhood has influenced your opinions about children, families, and being a parent?

3: HOW DO YOU FEEL ABOUT PREGNANCY AND CHILDBIRTH?

"I swear it traumatized me to this day. I haven't had children, and now I can't look at anything to do with childbirth. It absolutely disgusts me."
-Dame Helen Mirren, an Oscar-winning actress, on how she was traumatized by an educational childbirth film when she was a 13-year-old girl to explain why she is firmly against having children.

In this step, we are going to take a look at your feelings and thoughts about pregnancy and childbirth. Some women have a fear of pregnancy and childbirth, but don't realize it. They may think that their aversion to pregnancy and childbirth is an indication that they don't want to have children when really they are afraid of the process of having a child. These fears aren't giving them the chance to really assess whether or not they want to be a mother. They get blocked by thoughts of horrible pregnancies and delivery stories. Other women may want to have a child, but their fear may cause them confusion because of the conflicting feelings they have and they may ultimately avoid having them. This section will help you learn more about these fears and whether they are affecting your decision.

Tokophobia describes the fear of childbirth, coming from the Greek word for childbirth, tokos. It is also used to describe the fear of pregnancy. However, the formal word for fear of pregnancy is maieusiophobia.

There are two types of tokophobia:

- Primary tokophobia is the fear and deep-seeded dread of childbirth which pre-dates pregnancy and can start in adolescence or early adulthood. It often has to do something they learned in school, witnessed on television, or relates back to their own mother's experience.

- Secondary tokophobia is due to a previous horrendous experience regarding traumatic birth, poor obstetric practice or medical attention, postpartum depression, or other such upsetting events, which renders them emotionally unable to have more children. [1]

Medical professionals have said if women don't overcome their fear of childbirth, many remain childless or adopt. Or if they experience secondary tokophobia, they will avoid another pregnancy completely.

When I interviewed women to help me in making my decision whether or not to have a child, I encountered several that more than likely had tokophobia, although I didn't know it at the time. Many of them explained to me that one of the main reasons why they didn't want to have a child was because they couldn't bear the thought of being pregnant or giving birth. Here are some of the comments I heard:

"I couldn't imagine being pregnant and having a little alien thing living inside me. It just seems so gross. Like some kind of parasite living off a host and is going to eat through my stomach."

"The whole thought of being pregnant creeps me out. I get nauseas thinking about it."

"I was with my sister when she gave birth, and there was a lot of damage because she is so petite. She needed a lot of stitches. I can't get that picture out of my mind."

Other comments that have been reported in identifying tokophobia are:

"The truth is that the very thought of having something almost alien-like growing inside me is disgusting."

"It's not too strong to say that the very thought of childbirth disgusts me in a big way."

"It's much more than an anxiety - I am actually physically repulsed by pregnancy and childbirth."

"I even struggle to be around friends when they are pregnant and can't bear to watch or listen to anything about the process of having a baby."[2]

My experience

Although I was never formally diagnosed with tokophobia, I truly believe it was one of the reasons why I avoided having a child for so long. I couldn't imagine myself pregnant, and I never wanted to go through a birth experience. I felt that my body wasn't made for it. And, childbirth seemed traumatic.

I also had horrible menstrual cramps throughout my life, where I would sometimes be carried into the emergency room and given morphine. So when some friends and people I interviewed would tell me that contractions felt like very strong menstrual cramps, I knew it was something I wanted to avoid. I don't handle pain very well.

A dear friend of mine sensed my apprehension and thought that if I watched a child being born, it would be such an emotional experience for me that I would get over my fear. She and her husband were kind enough to let me witness the birth of their baby girl. I will admit being there made me more comfortable about the birthing process. But, I still couldn't imagine myself doing it.

It wasn't until I actually learned that I was pregnant that I immediately set up interviews with doctors who would give me an elective c-section. I met with 5 different doctors and went to 10 doctor's appointments until I found someone. It was quite stressful, but somewhere deep inside, I knew I could not give birth any other way. Little did I know at the time, that tokophobics usually request elective c-sections.

QUESTION:

What are your thoughts on pregnancy and childbirth? Do you have any extreme or adverse reactions?

4: DO YOU HAVE A MATERNAL INSTINCT?

One main concern I heard from women during my interviews, when they were trying to decide whether or not to have a child, was that they didn't feel any "maternal instinct" – that desire to have, care for, and even like a child. They say they don't get all warm or gooey inside when they are around children. They wonder if that is an indication that they are not mother material and shouldn't have children.

Understanding the terms

First, we need to get clear on a few terms that always get thrown around – biological clock, baby fever, maternal instinct. Some women say they feel their biological clock ticking. This a term that refers to the length of a woman's fertile potential, or the amount of time that a woman has to bear children – from puberty to menopause. So if a woman's biological clock is influencing a woman's decision to have a child, what she really means is that she realizes she has only so much time to have a child and she is feeling the pressure of that time period.

If a woman mentions that whenever she sees a baby or holds a baby, she feels a tug in her uterus or some other yearning physical or emotional sensation, or that she just has a strong longing for a baby, she is likely experiencing baby fever. Some women start to experience baby fever when they are teenagers; for others, it can be a feeling that suddenly emerges at different or later times in life. There hasn't been any scientific research on the feeling, so no one really knows the cause of it or why and when it occurs. People who have experienced it say it can't be satisfied by caring for someone else's child. And some say that it's a strong urge that usually goes against common sense. Others say it can be triggered by age, falling in love, previous pregnancies, or peer pressure.

Maternal instinct is the ability of a woman or mother to shelter, protect, care for, and nurture a child. During my interviews, women have told me that they have always loved children, enjoy taking care of them and find it quite pleasurable being around them. They consider themselves maternal and admit they have this instinct. Others told me that they do not like being around kids and do not enjoy taking care of them.

When deciding whether to have a child, the big issue concerning maternal instinct arises when a woman feels that she doesn't have such an instinct. She wonders if that means she isn't capable of mothering or thinks it's an indication that she shouldn't have children. She also wonders whether this maternal instinct will kick in if she does decide to have a child. And, she worries about what happens if it doesn't.

What women want to know about maternal instinct is whether it is an inherent trait that all women have or is it an ability that can be developed and learned. It appears that they want to use this quality as some kind of character marker or sign to help them determine if they are mother material. The reasoning goes something like this. If maternal instinct is an inherent trait in all women, but they don't have it or feel it, then that indicates or proves that they shouldn't have children. Or, if it isn't an inherent trait, then they want some reassurance these nurturing feelings will be able to develop within them once they have a child.

Is maternal instinct innate or learned?

"Instinct" is the inherent inclination of a living organism toward a particular behavior. It may differ depending on what field of science is using the term. Early on in biology, "instinct" was used to describe a fixed action or pattern without variation that did not require thought or consciousness to perform – it was automatic. Every specimen of a particular species would have to have it for it to be considered an instinct.

In psychology, experts use "drives" and "motivational forces" rather than "instinct" because it is believed that humans have the ability to override an instinct. Sociologists also don't believe humans have instincts because humans have the ability to override sex and hunger – two behaviors that are thought of as instinctual.

Those who claim that maternal instinct is not innate usually justify their position by pointing out the obvious—that many women in the world say they don't have or feel a maternal instinct and, therefore, don't have children

Sarah Blaffer Hrdy, a professor emeritus of anthropology and author of *Mother Nature: A History of Mothers, Infants and Natural Selection*, explains in her book that the desire to care for a child depends on a woman's desire to be a mother and the amount of time she spends bonding with her child. She says that maternal responses exist, and she believes they are biologically conditioned, but they are not true instincts. She believes that they develop as a mother spends time caring for her child.

However, with the advance of science, experiments can now be conducted that can test genes, hormones, neurotransmitters, and brain activity to explain the physiology and biology of our behaviors. Because of these tests, some believe that maternal abilities are hard-wired or more innate.

One of the first tests involved the manipulation of "early" genes crucial in learning and memory. These genes were altered in female rats, causing them to ignore their own infant pups, which ended up dying from neglect. The researchers were quick to caution against using the test results as indicative of human behavior. [1] But, the research was intriguing because it made people wonder if people had a genetic predisposition toward mothering, as well.

More recently, researchers conducted tests to see whether there was a genetic influence on the sensitivity of parenting. They found that less sensitive parents did have certain serotonin (happiness hormone) and oxytocin (the hormone of love and bonding) system genes. Mothers with oxytocin OXTRAA or AG genotypes were less sensitive than mothers with the GG genotypes. And mothers with serotonin 5-HTT ss were less sensitive than mothers with 5-HTT sl or ll.[2]

In their report, the researchers pointed out that the influence of genetic differences in 5-HTT and OXTR is much smaller than the association between sensitive parenting and parental education level. They wrote that "lower maternal education level is more strongly associated with less sensitive parenting than genes potentially related to less efficient oxytocin production."

In 2009, researchers at Tufts University Veterinary School conducted tests with virgin and nulliparous rats – rats that never bore children – and determined that these rats exhibited maternal behavior to pups that were not their own. Researchers exposed virgin rats to foster pups daily until they began to take care of the pups and show maternal behavior. They discovered that new neurons formed in the brains of these virgin rats. They weren't sure if the neuron growth came from the hormones produced by the virgin rat or stimulation from the young pups. Similar tests have shown that exposure to young stimulates maternal behavior in mice, hamsters, monkeys, and even humans. [3]

Another test showed that mothers have an intrinsic and visceral tie to their children. At the Medical University of South Carolina, researchers showed that the activity in a mother's brain was more widespread in reaction to cries from their infant than from cries of unrelated infants.

A similar test was conducted in Tokyo. Researchers wanted to see if mothers reacted differently to their children, compared to unrelated children. They videotaped the babies smiling at their mothers during playtime and then videotaped the children crying for their mothers to come back. All the babies were dressed the same. The mothers' brains were scanned with MRIs as they watched their babies play and then cry. When a mother saw images of her own child crying, her brain patterns were very different than when she watched other children.[4]

It's important to remember that we all have a unique genetic disposition. This biological foundation is influenced and affected by our environment – our families and other social connections, as well as our emotions and thoughts that we experience in reaction to our environment. "Hard-wired" from a genetic perspective is not a trait that is fixed and unchanging. It's just a trait whose potential for development is programmed by our genes. It may unfold in the context of various environmental scenarios.

So, depending on your genetic make-up, which is unique to you, different experiences—like getting an education, falling in love, being around children, having a child, focusing on your work and a career—can affect your biology. Some experiences may bring out our maternal tendencies; some may not. Our brains can change, depending on what environments and situations we are exposed to and the experiences we have.

How maternal drives affect our decision to have a child

Women who know they have maternal tendencies and a desire for children still may need to decide whether or not they want to have children. Some may still choose to remain childfree. They may feel and know that they have the emotional capabilities to relate to and take care of a child, but they may decide that is not something they want to do. Some women I spoke to who knew they had a maternal instinct and decided not to have children did so because they worked with children already and took pleasure in that. And some felt that although they had the capabilities had other interests they wanted to pursue.

For those who don't believe they have those maternal drives or urges, they wonder if that's an indication that they shouldn't have a child. They think that if they have no maternal drive, it must be an indication that they don't "want" a child. Others are concerned that if they don't have any maternal interest now, and they still go ahead and have a child, what if their maternal tendencies don't develop after they give birth? Many women who lack these maternal feelings don't want to risk it.

In Lara Scott's book, *Two is Enough: A Couple's Guide to living Childless by Choice*, she says, "I had no desire, no longing, to have a child to call my own. Rocking a child to sleep or breastfeeding an infant held no appeal to me, and on the few occasions when I did hold an infant in my arms, I felt awkward and inept. I had decided that 'Mom' was not a role I was well suited for, much the same way I'd determined I would never be a mathematician or a veterinarian."

Seventy-five percent of the childfree women (out of 100) Lara Scott surveyed for her book said they were strongly motivated to remain childfree because they "have no desire to have a child, no maternal/paternal instinct." These people considered themselves "hardwired" not to have kids.

However, there are women who said they had no maternal instinct whatsoever and still had children and loved being mothers. Here is what Erin, a 33-year-old account representative, shared with me:

"Before I had my own child, I was the least maternal person around. My friends and I would actually make fun of people with children, and we avoided them as much as possible. Their lifestyles seemed so boring, and we were so happy to have our freedom. I never got misty-eyed or cooed over babies. I never babysat – not once – and never changed a diaper. When people would ask me to babysit, I would always make excuses. When a friend did become pregnant, our relationship usually grew distant as I couldn't imagine why she'd want to have a baby."

"Then I did get pregnant with my husband, and it wasn't planned. I didn't feel maternal when I found out I was pregnant and was wondering what I was going to do. But when I went for a sonogram and saw my baby, it was if a maternal button was pushed inside me somewhere and I changed. I am so maternal now and love to make my son my main priority. Everything about him means more to me than anything. And, although I used to be a career-oriented person, I stay at home with him. I've become, 'one of them – those people with the boring life,' but none of that matters. What matters is that I look forward to seeing my son grow and develop. I'm in it for life. I want to be a good mother to help him develop into a young man, and I'll always be there for him."

But there is no guarantee that your maternal ability will kick in after you have a child. There are stories of women who, for a variety of reasons, aren't capable of bonding with or loving their child, even after giving birth. The Internet contains many testimonials of women who will admit that even after having children, they have no maternal capabilities. Some have even said they have never been able to relate to their children, and some even don't like them.

I have interviewed several women who have shared with me their stories of pain growing up as children with mothers who just couldn't relate, bond or love them. Many went through therapy to deal with their unaffectionate and distant mothers. Some have cobbled together relationships as adults with their mothers; others have found mother substitutes or built a new family among friends. Some had to cut off all ties with their birth mother in order to cope with the hurt they had experienced. This is one of my main motivators in writing this book. To help men and women decide it they truly want children and are willing to work at the relationship. The negative effect parents can have on children is devastating.

My story

In my case, I didn't have any maternal instinct before I had my son. I never wanted to have children when I was younger. I told everyone that I'd never have a child and that I'd never be married. I also had a mother who was distant and not very nurturing toward me, and who was uncomfortable showing me affection. She told me many reasons why not having children was a better alternative to having them. I also had a father who didn't know how to relate to me very well and wasn't very involved in my life. I spent many years obtaining a higher education and working in corporate settings that were devoid of children. And, I spent little time with young ones in general. At one time I mistakenly bought a squeeze dog toy for a baby shower gift. (It looked like one of those teething things that babies bit on.) I was maternally handicapped.

When I found out I was pregnant, I was quite concerned about how my pregnancy and the birth of my child would play out. I knew I was going to have this baby, and yet, I had no experience. I decided to stay open-minded and have no expectations. My only thought was to take it one day at a time and be mindful of my feelings and actions. What gave me hope was I remembered that when I was younger, I had dogs that I enjoyed caring for and I thought that just maybe I did have it in me to care for another living being.

What I was certain about, was that I wanted to raise my child differently than my mother and father raised me. I wanted my child to feel loved, safe, and secure. It is very painful for a child not to feel loved by a parent. However, after my child was born, I didn't feel a rush of loving emotion. I did feel love, but it was a more distant kind of appreciation that he was born healthy. For the first few days and weeks, I kept my focus on how to heal from my delivery and the day-to-day routine of taking care of my son – feed, diaper change, nap, feed, diaper change, nap. I didn't care about friends, extended family, or work. Nothing else was as important.

My husband also helped, which was of great comfort. Once we were so tired we slept through the night and woke up refreshed, as if we didn't have a child. We rushed to our son's crib next to the bed to make sure everything was alright because he didn't wake up in the middle of the night or we were just so exhausted we didn't hear him. We were so thankful to see him sleeping and thought *what a great kid to let his parents get some rest.*

About three weeks into my new life, I was in a robe standing over the stove cooking something, wondering, "How did I get here?" And, I glanced over at my son in his bouncy chair on the table to make sure he was okay. My eyes locked onto his eyes, and I felt this immense rush of love that brought tears to my eyes. Without sounding maniacal, in that moment, I actually thought I saw the love of God beaming at me through the eyes of my child. It was so powerful. I felt so much love for him that I couldn't stop crying. It was as if my heart was cracked opened—as if scar tissue that had built up through the

67

years finally melted, and I was free to feel the most intense love that I have ever felt. To this day, and as I write this, tears still come to my eyes, and I am so profoundly thankful that I was allowed to love like this.

From that moment on, I have had more compassion and empathy –for children and humanity. Before I had my son, it was never easy for me to cry. I always felt I needed to be in control, be strong, be tough. Now, I can go to a grocery store, see a child sitting in a cart, and weep at the beauty of his or her existence. I now cry at commercials and when my son draws me a picture. Emotionally, I have been transformed.

However, I still acknowledge that motherhood doesn't come easy to me. I think I have a great connection with my son. I love him freely and unconditionally, and I enjoy being with him. At times, I miss him when he's not around. But, when he was younger, I had to make a conscious effort to slow down and pay attention. As he gets older, it's much easier to communicate and he's more self-sufficient. I have to remind myself to be patient when we play games, and there are times when I have to force myself to stay in the moment and listen. As my son's interests become more diverse and not just focused on our immediate family (yes, I am now boring mom), and we both start venturing out into the world, I want to make sure that I keep my heart open.

What to do if you don't have a maternal instinct

If you don't have a maternal instinct, you may think it's an indication that you shouldn't have children or don't want children. It is possible that this is the case. You could have other interests, and maybe having a child isn't one of them.

In an *Elle* magazine article, a woman wrote about her struggles in deciding whether to have a child. Her friend told her, "If you have to give babies this much thought, and if you're this worried about being a mom, maybe that means you shouldn't become one."[5]

But, from a different perspective this could indicate sincere and possibly subconscious interest. As one of my friends said to me as I interviewed my 250th subject, "For someone who doesn't want kids, you sure are spending a lot of time talking, thinking, and asking a lot of questions about them."

However, if you think that you may want to have children even though you don't feel a strong maternal urge, you may want to consider what anthropologist Sara Blaffer Hrdy said in an interview with Salon.com:

"A woman who is committed to being a mother will learn to love any baby, whether it's her own or not; a woman not committed to or prepared for being a mother may well not be prepared to love any baby, not even her own."

People have advised women to go spend time with children to determine if they like being with children or if they feel like nurturing them. Personally, I don't think this is a good idea because I've met many women who told me that working at a day care or being a nanny for a summer was one of the major factors that helped them decide NOT to have children. I know that I particularly didn't like babysitting.

I know there are women and men who enjoy working with children, and they want to have them. But I also know of women and men who enjoy working with children and like to "give them back" when they are done. I've also interviewed women who told me they didn't like or want to be around other people's children but did enjoy their own. So, I don't think hanging out with other people's kids may be a true indicator of whether or not you have a maternal instinct.

Dr. Sandra Wheatley, a psychologist in Britain who has worked with antenatal and postnatal depression, explained her view of maternal instinct in an interview with babyworld.co.uk. She said that an instinct is something you are inherently good at, but it doesn't have to be natural. It can be developed, like a skill at gardening or cooking. The more you practice, the better you get. It's the same with mothering; it is a skill that can be developed.[6]

She also said that a woman's expectation about having maternal instinct can cause her difficulty. She said that some women believe and expect to be perfect—that they should have this strong maternal urge from the beginning and know everything about their baby's needs. In reality, she said that taking care of babies and children is hard work because they don't come with operating instructions and can't tell us what they want. She believes it's unrealistic for mothers to think they have to understand and know everything about their children at all times. And, that mothers who may not have an easy time understanding or relating to a baby's needs may be better at relating to their child at different stages of development, Mothers who are realistic about their own limitations and behaviors from the start may have an easier time with motherhood.[7]

And, I agree. From my own experience, I think it takes time to get used to a new role and a desire to have a relationship with your child. And, an openness and willingness for personal growth and change helps, as well.

QUESTIONS:

Do you have a maternal instinct? If not, do you have an interest in being a mother? If you had a child, would you be committed and willing to learn how to be a mother and take care of your child? Have you ever had to learn

something new which you may not have liked every aspect or it or were good at it in the beginning, but through time and effort came to develop a certain level of competency?

5: FACTORS THAT ARE INFLUENCING YOUR DECISION

Age

Is your decision being influenced by your age? Some of the women I interviewed have imaginary deadlines in their minds about what they would like to accomplish and by when. Some mentioned that they wanted to have all their children before they are 30. Some said they wanted to start having kids when they are 30. Some said if they reach 35 and haven't met the right person yet, they will have a child on their own. Others said 40 is when they will decide to have children. Do you have an age deadline?

As mentioned earlier, the average age for first births in the United States is 24.9. In other developed countries, the age is 27 to 29. However, the age is lower in the United States because we have a higher rate of teenage pregnancies than other developed countries, which pulls down the age. If teenage pregnancies weren't factored in, the average age for first births in the United States is the same as other developed countries, 27 to 29. So if you are in this age group, it's probably natural that you are wondering about whether or not to have a child, since this is an age when many women have their first child.

Some of our age deadlines are relevant since so much or our biological development correlates with our age, such as fertility. As the medical community likes to remind us, as a woman ages, her fertility declines. When a woman is in her teens and twenties, she has a 20 to 25% chance to get pregnant each month. When she's 30, she has a 20% chance. When she's 40, there is only a 5% chance.

In my case, I really didn't consider having a child until I was in my early 30s. I was too busy with school, working, and being in my relationship. However, when I started to have thoughts about whether I wanted to have a child, I told myself that I would make my decision by the time I was 40 since it seemed that fertility became more of an issue. As it turned out, I had my son when I was 39½ years old.

Relationship

How is being or not being in a relationship affecting your decision? According to a recent study, 50% of parents said that the reason they had a child was because their spouse or partner wanted one.[1] When in a relationship, we cannot help but be influenced by the person that we care about and love. We feel good when we are around them, which can influence us to look at the world differently and be open to other experiences. We may feel that this is a person we could have a child with because they make us feel safe and secure, or they have that special "something" that makes you feel that they "are the one."

I've interviewed men who told me how they never felt like settling down and having a family until they met their wife, or mother of their child. And, I've met women who said that they didn't want to have a child unless they met the right person. They said they felt they couldn't handle raising a child by themselves and felt that having a child was an endeavor that should be experienced with someone who also wanted to bring a child into the world. They felt a child deserved two parents. They also felt that having a partner for emotional support and helping with childcare would make the experience better.

Other situations involve couples where one person wants a child more than the other. In these cases, one of the partners usually acquiesces. Where one partner wants a child, the other may go along with that person's wishes to make them happy. Where one partner doesn't want to have a child, the other partner may go along because they value the relationship more than the experience of having a child in their lives.

Some women I've met who are in relationships start to think about whether they want to have children, because being in the relationship sometimes makes them wonder "what next?" Where is this relationship going? They start thinking about children to figure out the next steps to the relationship's progression. For example, some women feel if they figure out what whether or not they want a child, then they will ask their partner to see what he thinks. If they decide to have a child and their partner doesn't, then they may decide to end the relationship. Or if they decide they don't want to have a child, then once again, they will see what their partner's position is to determine the future of the relationship. But keep in mind, are you really trying to assess whether or not you want a child, or are you using the decision to have a child to get more out of a relationship or to get out of one?

Realizing your decision whether to have a child can be influenced by your relationship and your partner, you may want to consider if that person wasn't in your life, would you still want a child? Or not?

Family

When people think about having children, they also may want to consider how their extended family is influencing their decision to make sure a child is something they really want in their life and not due to influences of parents or siblings. Some people came from great families and want to have a child and create that same wonderful experience for their child. You should also be aware if you are being influenced from the opposite extreme – that you grew up in a dysfunctional family and don't want to have a family because you don't want to pass on that dysfunction to future generations.

I have heard many stories about how immediate and extended family members have provided input or made comments about a person's decision to have a child. The typical comment I hear is that once a couple becomes married, family members start asking about when they are going to have children, assuming that is the natural progression in a relationship. In my case, I wasn't even married when I received the comments. I dated my husband for about eight months before I met his parents and was starting my second year of law school. Within 15 minutes of talking to his mother (the mother of four children), she asked me if working in law would allow me to stay at home with my children when I had them or if I could work from home. The question caught me off guard, especially since I was only dating her son and was, at that point in time, clearly in the "No marriage, no kids" point in my life.

After being married to my husband for several years, I was in Chicago for business and thought I'd invite my mother-in-law to tea to try to connect with her and do something special. She came in happy and smiling and brought pictures to show me of her other grandchildren. We talked for a while and she asked me, "Do you have something to tell me?" It was then that I realized that she thought I had invited her to tea to tell her I was pregnant—which I wasn't, and wasn't even close to figuring out. When I told her that I wasn't pregnant, she was obviously crestfallen. I felt then that maybe she thought we could connect better if I had a child, and it wasn't happening.

Others have shared with me their parent's comments. Mainly I hear that parents will not say much or say that it's up to their grown child to make that decision for themselves. Parents realize that having and raising a child is a lot of responsibility and not always easy, so they want their children to make the best decision for themselves. They will be loved and accepted either way – with grandchildren or without.

Some other interview subjects said that their parents started vocalizing their desire for grandchildren once their friends and peers start becoming grandparents. Others have shared that their parents have encouraged them by offering them financial incentives—money to cover costs of childcare, help to pay off student loans, down payments on houses, college tuition trust funds, and even lump sum amounts. Potential future grandparents have also offered their services, saying that they will help with childcare or offering to watch the child a week every quarter so the parents can have time or a vacation for themselves. One professional baseball player has put together a trust for his daughter giving her a six-figure sum every year she stays at home with her children, so she doesn't have to worry about money or work.

But some people I interviewed shared how their parents encouraged them not to have children. These people were told that children are a lot of work and that they should enjoy their freedom. Some parents told their kids, "Anyone can have a kid. Isn't there something else you'd want to do?" Some parents told their children that if they had to do it again, they probably would've been happy not having children.

In my case, I didn't want to have children because I didn't feel that I had the best childhood or that I even knew how to be a mother. Motherhood wasn't something that was encouraged or admired in my family. My husband felt that, although he had a decent childhood, he had a very difficult relationship with his parents as an adult. So, we both were against bringing a child into this world who may not be treated well or kindly by our families. Not having children was our way of preventing unnecessary hurt. What I learned over time, though, was that even though this was our background, the lives we create moving forward could be different.

Is your actual family giving you hints or encouragement about having children? Our extended family can have a strong influence on us. Our families have their own set of unspoken rules that we learn by living with them. Does your family value having children? Do your parents ever mention that you should have or not have children? Do your parents comment about siblings who have or don't have children? What messages are you getting from your family?

Friends

How are your friendships influencing you? I've been told by some women that they never thought about having children until their best friend had a child.

When it comes to friends and pregnancy, the conversation many times turns to teenage pregnancy as we hear in the news about girls in high schools making "pregnancy pacts" or the tendency in some schools for teenage girls becoming pregnant after one of them does. We also have more reality TV shows that bring the lives of teenage mothers into our living rooms. And these teen moms are glamorized and treated like celebrities just because they are on TV. Three friends of one reality teen mom became become pregnant while she was on the show and some speculated that it was because of the "celebrity treatment" and attention the original teen mom received that influenced the other girls' pregnancies— although, they deny it.

But being influenced by friends isn't limited to teenage girls. Sometimes when we learn a friend is pregnant and has a child, it may cause us to wonder about our own situation. We may wonder if having a child is something we want or even can do. Other times, it can solidify our decision NOT to have a child when we see how their lives change.

On the flip side, one woman I interviewed wondered if her friends were influencing her in the opposite direction – to not have children. She said that most of her friends are childfree women and are outspoken about their negative views about children and motherhood. Two of her best friends espouse these views. She is concerned that she may be leaning toward not wanting children because she's worried she will lose their friendship if she did end up having children.

Religion

Is your religion influencing you?

"Be fruitful and multiply, and replenish the earth . . ."
(The Bible, Genesis 1:28)

"We declare that God's commandment for His children to multiply and replenish the earth remains in force."
(Latter Day Saints, *The Family: A Proclamation to The World*)

The Qur'an does not make any explicit statements about the morality of contraception, but contains statements encouraging procreation. The prophet Muhammad also is reported to have said "marry and procreate."[2]

For many people, their religion is part of their identity, and they live their lives according to the tenants and practices that are spelled out in their holy texts and disseminated by their holy leaders. They are born into it through their families or feel drawn to it by their own spiritual yearnings. Studies have shown that people who believe in more traditional religions that encourage family values tend to have more children. More teenage pregnancies occur in states that have religious populations. And, many Mormons and Catholics have larger families.

I interviewed a 41-year-old woman in Michigan with nine children who said that her belief in Catholicism was the main factor that motivated to have so many children. I also interviewed a Mormon woman who had nine siblings, but had only one child herself. She said that growing up in a large family and with a religion that encouraged procreation had the opposite effect on her. She opted for a smaller family. So your religious beliefs don't necessarily have to determine whether you have children or the amount you have.

I grew up in a large Catholic family and was raised going to church on Sundays, and even Saturdays. Through the years, I stopped going to church. Yet, I still remain spiritual and believe in God. But I don't feel that I need a religion in order to worship. For me, organized religion is a path that others may choose to practice. But, I believe the underlying purpose of all religions is to lead us all to the same place—a relationship with God. So even though I was raised in a large extended family, I didn't feel compelled to have one of my own.

QUESTION:

How may your age, relationship, family, friends and religious beliefs be influencing your decision?

6: WRITE IT OUT

Take some time to write out your answers to the questions we addressed in this section to understand what your current thoughts and feelings are about having a child.

1. Why are you thinking about having a child now?
2. What was your childhood experience?
3. How do you feel about pregnancy and childbirth?
4. Do you have a maternal instinct? If not, do you have an interest in being a mother? If you had a child, would you be committed and willing to learn how to be a mother and take care of your child?
5. How may your age, relationship, family, friends and religious beliefs be influencing your decision?

STEP TWO

TOP 12 FACTORS
TO CONSIDER

STEP 2 - TOP 12 FACTORS TO CONSIDER

There are hundreds of questions and issues a person could ponder when deciding whether to have a child. And there are just as many answers and information found in resources in books, magazines, and on the Internet that can overwhelm and distract you. Just thinking about one subject, such as "How will having a child affect my career?" could illicit a multitude of "what if" scenarios that could cause a person to over-think an issue and get stuck. For example, thinking "How will having a child affect my career?" could lead to:

If I have a child, will I want to continue working?

How would my supervisor react to me?

Will I still be taken seriously?

Would I still be given interesting assignments?

Will I be able to do my job at the level I'm used to?

How has my company supported new moms in the past?

Should I look for another position within the firm that is more flexible?

Can we survive on my husband's salary alone if I decide to stay home?

Can we afford childcare if I return to work? Is it worth it?

The questions can go on and on. As I explained in earlier chapters, over-thinking an issue isn't going to be helpful. In order to avoid this possibility, in this section I am going to share with you the Top 12 Factors that people usually consider when deciding whether to have a child.

When I interviewed people to help me with my own decision, it seemed that the same subjects kept coming up: Finances, Career, Relationships, Regrets, to name a few. Of course, my interviewees weren't concerned about all these factors. Usually, only a few stood out for them, depending on their situation. By reviewing these Top 12 Factors and the research and information I have gathered, you can better identify which ones are pertinent to your situation.

At the end of each Factor, I ask thought-provoking questions, not necessarily to help you come up with a definitive answer that you would act upon, but to help you think of your position from a different perspective. By doing this, these questions can help you determine whether that Factor is truly a concern for you, or if you are possibly using it as an excuse for a deeper issue that you may not realize or may be reluctant to face. When I was contemplating my decision, my friends and family asked me these types of questions. My answers helped me realize which factors were an issue for me, and which ones I didn't need to resolve.

I am hopeful that the information I provide for each Factor will help answer your questions or help you view the Factor from a different perspective in order to alleviate or resolve the concern you have so you can move forward in your decision making. If the Factor is one that is too confusing to sort out on your own, seeking insight and guidance from a counselor or therapist is highly suggested.

1. POPULATION:
Are there too many people in the world?

Depending on a person's values, population is a concern for some when deciding whether to have a child. When I interviewed people who were leaning toward not having children or already decided not to, one reason they often cited is that the world is overcrowded and they did not want to contribute to over population and the environmental repercussions that stem from it. Some believed they were being altruistic in saving the planet and contributing to the betterment of humanity. Others who did decide to have a child, or already had one, explained that they limited the amount of children they were considering or already had due to population concerns.

I've provided the most recent population data for you to consider. It may be surprising to learn that, although world population is growing, it's not due to people having more children—it is due to people living longer. And the number of children being born per woman (fertility rate) in most developing countries is falling.

On average, the world population is getting older, and fewer children are being born. It is predicted that within 20 years, Europe and Asia will face the situation where a majority of their populations will be over 65 and the average age will be approaching 50.[1] This "graying" of country populations has some governments worried since fewer children being born mean there are less people to support the social programs for the older, retired generation. These countries have implemented natalist policies to help encourage people to have children.

While some people consider the overall world population and decide not have children, the reduction in fertility rates in certain industrialized countries have influenced others to have children. Some countries offer financial incentives and other "freebies" under pro-natalist policies to encourage people to have children. Some living in these countries feel justified and even patriotic to contribute to their country's population. Others who feel that their race is in decline feel they are adding to the cultural diversity of the planet by having children and are making a contribution to humanity by doing so.

Although we hear that global population is an issue, we may not know the details. This section reveals the data of the population globally and in major countries to help you put your decision in perspective.

Interviews

Wendy is a 35-year-old accountant who is married to Yoichi, a 32-year-old Internet entrepreneur. They both are socially progressive and care about the world. They are vegan, drive electric cars, and, when the U.S. invaded Iraq, they both decided that they'd return to Yoichi's hometown in Japan. They have traveled extensively throughout the world and are cognizant of environmental issues.

"I think that many of our environmental problems stem from overpopulation, and I don't really want to be a contributor to a problem. I'd rather be a solution. Which means, by not having children, I feel like I'm contributing to making the world a better place," Wendy told me during our interview.

Yoichi added, "When we considered our decision to have children, the main factor for us was the state of the world we live in. We didn't think it was a healthy or positive environment to raise a child in. We felt that there were too many people already. It makes us feel good not to be having a child. We feel we are doing something positive by not having them."

Sabina is a Ph.D. candidate and working on a fellowship in Berlin, Germany, documenting certain historical aspects about the Holocaust. While in Germany, she met and became engaged to a German man. She told me that prior to meeting her husband, she didn't want to have children. The work she is involved in forces her to constantly focus on the atrocities committed by humanity, and she had a rather negative view of the future of the world. She said she didn't want to subject another human being to such a horrible world. However, meeting her fiancé and falling in love has given her hope about humanity. She also said that she has learned more about the population decline in Germany through her husband, and she doesn't feel that having a child would be contributing negatively to the world. She believes that having a child would help maintain Germany's population and views this as a positive contribution to humanity.

The global population is growing

When people say they don't want to have children because there are too many people in the world, if they consider over 6 billion people too much, they may be right. Currently, the global human population is just over 6.9 billion people.[2] It is estimated that there were about 1.6 billion people at the beginning of the 1900s and reached 6 billion in October 1999.[3] It is predicted that by 2012, there will be 7 billion people on the planet, and by 2050, the world's population will be (at the high end) 9.2 to 10.6 billion.[4] However, there are estimates that are higher and lower.

I have often wondered if human beings naturally regulate their population levels this way—that somehow we internally recognize that there are too many people and some of us naturally and intuitively decide not to have children based on our observations.

In 2000, the United Nations estimated that the world's population grows at a rate of 1.14% per year or about 75 million people per year. That is a decline of its peak at 2.19% in 1963. So, the world population is growing, but it's growing at a slower rate.

The five most populated countries are:

China – 1.343 billion
India – 1.210 billion
United States – 311 million
Indonesia – 238 million
Brazil – 194 million

China and India together account for 37% of the world's population, and all the countries comprising Asia account for 60% of the world population.

SOURCE: U.S. Census Bureau, International Database (IDB), Feb. 2011

Falling fertility rates is the trend

Although the global population is growing, the cause isn't because people are having more children – it's because people are, in general, living longer. Fertility rates, which is the average number of children women have over their lifetime, have been declining in many developed countries. The amount of births is not replacing the amount of people dying. Close to half the world's population now lives in countries with fertility rates below the replacement level – which is about 2.1 per woman. But, developed countries account for less than a fifth of the world's population. The great majority of the world's population with sub-replacement fertility resides in low-income societies. The result of low fertility and low mortality rates today leads to an aging population tomorrow. If fewer young people are born, than the remaining population will be older.

So what is causing people to have fewer children? In industrialized countries, greater wealth of societies, education, and urbanization give people more options. When a society becomes wealthier, birth control is understood, becomes more accessible, and is more affordable. In developed countries, the costs of having children are often deemed very high because of education, clothing, feeding, and social amenities. Longer periods of time are now spent getting higher education, which causes women to have children later in life. It has been shown that female labor participation has a negative impact on fertility. And, mortality rates are low in developed countries because people are living in better conditions and have medical help and interventions, if needed.[5]

In the future, there will be a larger population of elderly people with a disappearance of children. For every man and woman to replace themselves, the birthrates should be 2.1 babies per woman. Yet 59 countries have levels below replacement levels. Twenty-six of the world's major countries have reported to the United Nations that they are worried about their low birthrate, and the world population clock will start winding back within 50 years.[6]

Demographers predict that between now and 2030 the global supply of potential workers is set to grow much more slowly than in the previous two decades and that the oldest segment of the conventionally defined working-age population (men and women between 50-64 years of age – is projected to account for nearly half of all global manpower. The increase in the world's working age (bet 15 and 64) population between 2010 and 2030 will be around 900 million people - 400 million fewer than over the past few decades. Over the past 20 years, the two greatest centers of manpower growth have been China and India. Sub-Saharan Africa, Bangladesh, and Pakistan will generate nearly half the growth in the world's working-age population. Those to experience shrinkage of their working-age populations are: China, Japan, countries in eastern and western Europe, and the former Soviet states.[7]

Perspective: Fertility rates around the world

China. In 1980, China launched its one-child family planning campaign. The country added about 12 million people per year since then, the equivalent of birthing the entire population of Greece or Belgium annually. But the policy seems to have slowed expansion with China claiming it has prevented 400 million births (more than the population of the U.S. and Canada combined). But, China now has 32 million more boys than girls under the age of 20, due to the illegal, but widespread, practice of sex-selective abortion. The U.S. Census Bureau puts China's total fertility rate at about 1.5 children per woman, or 30% below the level required for long-term population stability.

India. A recent census in India revealed that the country added 181 million new citizens from 2000 to 2010, making it home to 17% of the world's population, for a total of 1.21 billion, with more boys being born than girls – 914 girls for every 1,000 boys.[8] The northern part of India has fertility rates that are quite high, with women having four, five, or more children. The lower half is more aligned with more developed countries, and population growth will be slowing or ceasing.[9]

Japan. Japan has had the steepest and longest fertility falloff. Japan had begun reporting sub-replacement fertility in the 1950s and has had uninterrupted sub-replacement fertility since the early 1970s. In 2008, the country recorded around 40 percent as many births as it had 60 years earlier. Japan is currently estimated to be nearly 35% below the replacement level. But their improvements in public health have contributed to the average life expectancy of 83 years – higher than any other country in the world. Japan's population is projected to fall from 127 million to 114 million, a 10 percent decrease. The decline in working age population is to be from 81 million to 67 million, or a 17% decrease. By 2030, the median age will be above 52, with 30% of the population 65 or older.

Russia. Since 1992, deaths have outnumbered births by roughly 50%, or about 13 million, and official figures suggest that the country's population has shrunk by 5% - nearly 7 million people – from 148.6 million in 1993 to 141.9 million today. Life expectancy in Russia is low. Between 1965 and 2005, death rates for men in their late 20s to mid-50s virtually doubled. Between now and 2030, the U.S. Census Bureau projects that Russia's working age population will drop by 20 percent. Death levels for Russia's working-age population were 25 percent higher than those of India's.

Europe. Western Europe's population may grow just by 3% over the next 2 decades, with near zero growth by 2030. Germany and Italy are expected to experience population decline. Europe's median age will rise from 42 today to 46 by 2030. Despite population stagnation, Western Europe's 65-and-older population is set to rise by 40%, while its manpower is set to shrink by 12 million people.

Italy. In Italy, about 25% of women do not have children, while another 25% only have one child. The region of Liguria in northwestern Italy has the highest ratio of elderly-to-youth in the world. Genoa, one of Italy's largest cities, is declining faster than most European cities with a death rate of 13.7 deaths per 1,000 people, almost twice the birth rate of 7.7 births per 1,000 people in 2005. To counter this trend, the government has offered financial incentives to couples who have children and increase immigration. More than 30% of Italian males over the age of 30 live in homes owned by their parents. Some young men are saying it's due to low wages and high rents that are causing them to live at home.

Australia. When birth control became available, the birthrate dropped from 3.5 to 2.9 from 1961 to 1966 and continued to decline throughout the 1970s. Replacement level was reached in 1976. That rate continued to decline in the 1980s and 1990s. In 1990, it was at 1.9, but fell to 1.7 by 2005. Australia's population continued to grow due to immigration and baby boomers having children. In 2005, one in five Australian women who were at the end of their child-bearing years had not had children, and this is expected to rise to one in four women.

Population and fertility in the United States

In the United States, the current population is at around 311 million. Between 2000 to 2009, it grew 9.1%. It is set to grow by 20%, from 310 million to 374 million, between 2010 to2030. The U.S. population growth rate will match India's. The U.S. Census Bureau claims that the U.S. share of the global population is not set to shrink due to a higher fertility rate compared to other developed countries and its continuing influx of immigrants.

Right now the population breakdown in the United States by age is:

21.5 million or 6.9% under the age of 5

54.1 million or 24.3% of people are between 5 and 18 years old

195.3 million or 62.8% are between 18 and 65 years old

40.1 million or 12.9% are over 65 years old.

Or 75.6 million young people under the age of 18, compared to 235.4 adults over the age of 18.

In 2009, the demographic of the United States are:

79.6% of people were white

12.9% were black

1% American Indian and Alaska Native

4.6% Asian

.2% native Hawaiian or other Pacific Islander

15.8% Hispanic or Latino

1.7% Reporting two or more races

65.1% White persons, not Hispanic

U.S. Census Bureau, Nov. 4, 2010

Each year, there are approximately 4 million births in the United States and 2.4 million deaths. U.S. fertility dropped to less than replacement level fertility in 1972 and by 2002, had dropped to a record low. Replacement level fertility is 2.1 children per woman. During most of the 1970s and 1980s, women gave birth to fewer than 2 children on average. In 2000, births increased 3% over births in 1999—the third straight increase following nearly a decade of decline from 1990 through 1997. Now the average number of children born to women over a lifetime is 2.03, slightly below replacement level.

U.S. fertility is dramatically higher than almost all other developed countries. Europe's aggregate fertility rates vary between approximately 1.3 and 1.5, depending upon region. Japan is at 1.3.

Most recently, more babies were born in 2007 than in any other year in the nation's history. Then the recession hit and births fell 2.6% in 2009, even as the population grew.

> Number of births in the United States by year
>
> 4,136,000 in 2009
> 4,247,000 in 2008
> 4,300,000 in 2007

Developed countries offering pro-natalist policies to encourage people to have more children

One of the main reasons cited for very low-birth rates in developed countries is the low compatibility between the family and work.[10] It's difficult to have and raise children when people are working all the time. So certain developed countries that are experiencing very low fertility rates (1.3 or less) are offering pro-natalist programs to encourage people to have children. These programs range from one-off payments, tax breaks, extended, flexible work schedules, and subsidized day care. Some governments, like in Japan, have even enlisted large companies to submit plans to "foster new generations."

In Europe, the Nordic governments (Sweden, Norway, Finland, Iceland, Denmark) are the most progressive and have a long history of developing social policies to help people balance their work and family lives. In Sweden, each parent is entitled to 18 months leave, which is paid for by the government. Public day care is heavily subsidized and flexible work arrangements are common. Women with pre-school age children are entitled to reduce their working hours. In Norway, mothers are entitled to 12 months work off with 80% pay or for 10 months with full pay. Fathers are entitled to take almost all of that leave instead of the mother. Fathers must take at least four weeks leave or else those weeks will be lost for both parents. The result is that birth rates are some of the highest in Europe, with 1.75 for Sweden and 1.81 in Norway.

In the UK, new mothers get six months paid leave and the option for another six months unpaid leave. The first six weeks are at 90% pay and the next 20 at about 102.80 British pounds (US$ 166). The government offers free early education places, and parents with children under the age of six have the right to ask employers for more flexible working hours.

Germany has had one of the lowest birth rates in Europe at 1.37 and in 2005 30% of German women have not had children. The government hasn't done much to address their low fertility rates until recently. Now, the government offers 14 weeks of maternity leave, plus parental leave up to 36 months. And in 2007 the government offered tax breaks to families. It also does offer free college or at a reduced cost, so that students aren't tied to a large debt when they finish.

France has the second highest fertility rate in Europe at 1.9 and has one of the most extensive state-funded child care systems. Mothers can take 16 weeks paid maternity leave for the first child, rising to 26 weeks for the third child. There is also total of 26 months of parental leave. In 2005, the government pledged more money for families with 3 children to encourage working women to have more children. Larger families get free museum passes and subway fares. Childcare facilities are subsidized by the government and younger children are entitled to full-day childcare.[11]

Eastern Asia countries, such as Japan, Singapore, and Korea, have focused more resources on encouraging their populations to have more children over the past ten years. Every few years, Singapore adds on more benefits: tax relief, child allowance, baby bonus programs, and prolonged maternal leave. In Japan, there are child allowances, daycare services, 14 weeks maternity leave, and 66% paid wages during maternity leave. In 2003, the Next Generation Law required local governments and large companies to submit their own programs to foster new generations. Korea started its prenatal program in 2006 and offers contributions to daycare costs, rewarding larger families through tax and housing, improved childcare services, expanded maternity and childcare leaves, and assisting mothers' employment. Because the high cost of private educational costs in Korea is known to be the main factor of low fertility, they have also offered after-school programs and cyber-education programs to compete.

Thought-provoking question

When I was in law school, I studied environmental law and became aware of the realities of how certain types of companies and industrial behavior, as well as over-population, can impact our environment. Yet this wasn't an issue for me when I was making my decision. I felt if I focused my time and energy on living my life in ways that had less of an environmental impact and supported technological advances that could improve the situation, then I would be making a contribution to the betterment of the planet. I also felt that there was no way of knowing if a future child of mine would be one of the people to help invent or create more solutions to our environmental problems.

QUESTION:

In five years, through technology and progressive legislation, the world is on track to remedy most of its population and environmental issues. Would you consider having a child if you knew that the world's problems would be improving or remedied?

---

2. FINANCES:

Can We Afford a Child?

During my interviews, when I'd ask, "What should people, in general, consider when deciding whether to have children?" almost everyone answered, "They should be able to afford them." In the United States, it seems we are constantly thinking about money. It's just a natural reaction since most of the transactions in our lives require some form of payment. It seems there are fewer pleasures and experiences that we partake in these days that don't involve the transfer of money.

However, when I asked these same people (at least the ones who had children) much later, in the same interview, "What did YOU consider before having your child?" none of them said finances or money. Apparently, it seems that we have double standards. We want to make sure everyone else has enough money to take care of their children, but when it comes to our own decision, considering whether or not we can afford them seems to diminish the emotional value we place on the love we feel for our children and the relationship we have with them. Putting a price on our own children seems somehow wrong. Putting a monetary value on a life we cherish so dearly cheapens the relationship, the human experience.

As one respondent told me, "You can't put a price on a human life." And others told me, when shrugging off the finance question, "You do what you have to afford them. You cut back in other areas that aren't as important anymore."

When I asked people if they knew how much it costs to have a child, almost everyone said they didn't know exact numbers. Of course, the cost of having a child will be different because there are so many variables, but most people didn't sit down and figure out if they could afford a child as someone may do with a house or car payment. Only a few of my interview subjects informed me that they were actually saving money to have children. Many of them usually fit the children into their current lifestyle.

When contemplating your decision to have a child, you may learn how much it costs to raise a child, but it is more than likely you will do what most other people do, which is to make sure you can provide for the child's basic necessities, but overall, you and your child will adapt to your current financial situation. People make adjustments depending on their financial circumstances and figure out ways to make it work.

Interviews

Lydia, a 72-year-old mother of 3 and grandmother of 5 who lives in Texas, told me that in her day they never considered whether you could financially afford a child. "We usually had our children and then made the best of it. Today, there seem to be so many more costs with having a child. Our kids never had as many toys as the kids do today."

Debbie, a 32-year-old market research specialist who works from home, and her husband, Steve, a 30-year-old chemical engineer who lives in Tennessee, told me that they both knew they wanted to have children and started saving right after their wedding. They told me they put aside about $500 a month. "It's not for the cost of having a child. Our insurance will cover most of that. It's to give us flexibility in the future in case we want to take time off or hire really good childcare."

William, a 65-year-old school teacher in the Midwest, told me that he decided not to have children so that he could have enough money for his retirement. "As a teacher, I didn't have the highest salary, and I felt that I had to make a choice about what I could spend my money on. I worked with kids, so I knew that they were expensive."

David, 45-year-old real estate developer in Southern California with 3 children under the age of 9, said that he and his wife, who owns a physical therapy practice, never took the time to figure out how much it cost to have children. "Our focus is on making money and attaining a certain lifestyle. That may sound crass. But, we love what we do and do what we have to for our family."

What Does It Cost to Raise a Child?

There are many variables that go into determining the cost of raising a child from birth until graduation from high school or college. Depending on where you live, the cost of living can greatly increase the cost. Or conversely, living in a less expensive area can reduce your expenses.

As of 2009, it cost between $11,650 and $13,530 a year to raise a child in a two-child, married-couple family in the middle-income range, and approximately $222,360 to raise a child from birth to age 17 in the western part of the United States.[1] This includes costs for housing, transportation, food, clothing, health care, education, and "other" (toothbrushes, iPods, and books), but not college. According to the Babycenter.com calculator, it costs about $355,906, including the college years.

There are several "cost of having a child" calculators on the Internet that allow you to enter in variables, such as the year your child is born, where you live, your level of income, and the number of parents in your household, to determine a more accurate estimate for your personal situation.

Cost of Living Calculators

The USDA calculator **determines an annual** cost for up to six children, not including college. It also allows you to determine costs based on a two-parent or single-parent household and the region of the country in which you live and considers before-tax income. Their approach is that what you will spend taking care of your child is dependent upon a variety of factors. http://www.cnpp.usda.gov/calculatorintro.htm

The Babycenter.com calculator provides a total lifetime amount, including college costs, where you can select public or private college as a choice.
www.babycenter.com/cost-of-raising-child-calculator

According to the 2009 U.S. Department of Agriculture study, the amount spent by families in higher income groups was about twice as much the amount spent by families in the lowest income group. All income groups spend about the same on child necessities, such as food and clothing, but discretionary spending on childcare and education varied more.[2] The largest expenditures for children are: housing, childcare and education, food and transportation. Child expenses increase as the child ages.[3] Child-rearing expenses are highest in the urban Northeast, then the urban West and then Urban Midwest. Child-rearing expenses are lowest in the urban South and rural areas. [4]

Indirect costs are not easy to predict or calculate. For example, the money or investments you forfeit because of the presence of children, and time you could use doing something else instead of spending it with children. Women are more affected by these costs than men.

High dual-income couples have the most to lose when they broach the subject of having children. The person who elects to be the main caregiver, usually the woman, faces a double jeopardy. In periods away from work, or in diminished work obligations, a woman not only loses a large income, but also finds herself dependent on her partner.[5]

Does your financial situation affect your decision to have a child?

It has been shown that during economic difficulties, people tend not to have children. In a recent study, it was shown that births in the U.S. declined by 2% in 2008. People explained that they had lost jobs and health insurance and were in worse shape financially. Almost half of the surveyed women (44%) said that because of the economy, they wanted to reduce the number of children they have or delay their childbearing. Lower income women were more likely to report changes in their fertility than higher income women. Sixty-four percent of the women agreed with the statement, "With the economy the way it is, I can't afford to have a baby right now."[6]

Not having children when times get tough isn't a new phenomenon. There was also widespread poverty during the Great Depression during the 1930s when unemployment ranged from 15 to 20%. Many families struggled and worried about finances, which also caused them to put off having children. The U.S. fertility rate declined by nearly 20% from 1928 thru 1935.[7]

Yet, those who have jobs and are in upper-income levels still continue to have children, and are having more than average. In the past 10 years, the top-earning 1.3% of population has seen an uptick in families with three or more children. Twelve percent of upper-income women had three children or more in 2002, compared with only 3% in 1995.[8] And, the proportion of affluent American families with four or more kids increased from 7% in 1991 to 1996 to 11% in 1998 to 2004.[9]

How our loss-adverse brains may scare us from having a child

It seems that people may not consider the actual dollar amounts when it comes to having children since that would seem inappropriate – putting a value on human life. Yet it appears people consider their economic situation when deciding whether to have children since the U.S. population has dropped over the past few years due to the recession. But can the thought of how much it costs to have and raise a child potentially create negative thoughts or reactions about having one so as to influence us not to want one?

As I mentioned in the first section, it seems that our brains, especially the pre-frontal cortex – the more rational part – is sensitive to the price and cost of items. Experiments using MRI technology show how brains act when price and cost is a factor in purchases, which can affect our decision-making process.

When a person is contemplating the purchase of a product, a process occurs in their brain that scientists can actually observe to see if a person will actually make the purchase. When first exposed to a product, a person's nucleus accumbens

(NAcc) is turned on. The NAcc is a crucial part of the dopamine reward pathway, and the intensity of its activation shows how much a person desires an object. If the person wants the item, dopamine from the NAcc floods the brain when the item first appears. Then, when the cost of the product is shown, the insula and prefrontal cortex were activated. The insula produces adverse feelings and is triggered by things it interprets as painful – such as the spending of money – causing a person to avoid the thing. The prefrontal cortex is activated to compute the numbers, trying to figure out if the product is a good deal and gets excited when the price is lower than normal.

By measuring the relative amount of activity in each brain region, scientists can accurately predict a person's shopping decisions. They can tell which products people would buy before they did. If the insula's negativity exceeded the positive feelings generated by the NAcc, then the subject chose not to buy the item. If the NAcc was more active than the insula, or if the prefrontal cortex was convinced that it had found a good deal, the object was irresistible. The sting of spending money doesn't compare with the thrill of getting something new. When we make a purchasing decision, much of the calculation is done by our emotional brain, which relies on relative amounts of pleasure versus pain to tell you what to purchase. The emotion felt most intensely tends to dictate the shopping decision.

When it comes to thinking about having a child, one has to wonder if a similar emotional argument is going on inside the brain. The NAcc might want the baby, but the insula knows you can't afford it, or the prefrontal cortex rationalizes it out (cost vs. benefit) and realizes it is a bad deal. These conflicting emotions may manifest themselves as a twinge of uncertainty.

Does money really make us happy?

But should we place that much emphasis on money and finances when we think about having a child? Do we think that by having more money we will be happy?

There have been several studies conducted over the past few years to help us understand money and how it's tied to our happiness. When it comes to happiness, there are two types: our day-to-day level of happiness or emotional well-being that can change depending on what's going on in your life, and our overall life satisfaction which is a deeper, longer term feeling about how your life it turning out. Studies on happiness have shown that $40,000 to $90,000 is needed for our emotional well-being, and generally as a person's income rises, their overall sense of success increases.

One study conducted by Angus Deaton and Daniel Kahneman in 2010 at Princeton University found that people who made about $75,000 a year were happy, from a life satisfaction perspective. People who made more didn't report any greater degree of happiness. When people make more than $75,000, they feel like their life is going in a good direction, but they aren't necessarily more cheery on a daily basis. [10] "Giving people more income beyond $75K is not going to do much for their daily mood...but it is going to make them feel they have a better life," Deaton pointed out in an interview.[11]

Lower income only makes people feel badly about dealing with problems they already have, like health issues or divorce. When people make $75,000 it seems those troubles aren't as difficult to deal with. Researchers think that amount probably gives people enough money to deal with their problems more effectively, and they have extra money to do things that make them feel good.[12]

It has also been discovered that happiness is not about absolute wealth (how much you have in the bank and what you own), but relative wealth or status (how much you have compared to someone else). [13]

In a study conducted by the University of British Columbia and Harvard Business School, researchers asked over 429 people earning a broad range of incomes – from $5,000 to $200,000 – to rate their own happiness. Then they were asked to predict how happy they and others would be at different salary levels, both higher and lower. The results show that people overestimate how closely money and happiness are tied. For example, respondents predicted that people making $55,000 a year would rate their happiness at around 51% on a scale of 1 to 100 and that a person making $125,000 could expect a happiness rating of 73 out of 100. In reality, the $55,000 earners weighed in at 76 on the happiness scale, and those who make $125,000 were actually less happy, at around 68. [14]

Most surprising, however, was just how drastically respondents mis-rated the happiness of those who earn less. They predicted that people making $10,000 dollars a year would rate their happiness at a paltry 13 out of 100, and that a worker making $25,000 should only expect a happiness rating of 23 out of 100. In reality, the average $10,000 earner came in at a respectable 50 on the happiness scale, and the average person who makes $25,000 ranked their happiness at 70 out of 100 – nearly three times higher than the study subjects predicted. The only area where the participants' intuitions were correct was at the top of the income scale, where they rightly predicted that people making $1 million aren't much happier than those making $90,000. [15]

So what makes people happy?

Money doesn't bring enduring happiness. Humans adapt psychologically to their circumstance—including their monetary circumstances. People get used to what they earn and any economic gains and losses, which gives them pleasure or pain when they happen, but that effect fades. Adaptation makes money unsatisfying because we get used to it so quickly. An increase in income becomes the new normal. The logic stems from adaptation theory – when people experience a positive event, two effects take place. In the short run, well-being increases; and in the long run, people adjust to their new circumstances, which diminish the positive effect of the event. Economists refer to this tendency to adapt as the "hedonic treadmill."

Harvard psychology professor Daniel Gilbert says that once you have enough money to meet basic needs – food and shelter—incremental increases have little effect on your happiness. In his PBS documentary series, *This Emotional Life*, Gilbert explains the secrets to happiness, and it's not money. "

1) You can't be happy alone. Social relationships are the single most important ingredient of happiness. They are key.

2) You can't be happy all the time. We have to experience negative emotions as part of being human. But it's HOW we experience negative emotions that count.

3) You can be happier than you are. There are universal traits of happy people that you can implement to raise your happiness level."[16]

A large global survey of 136,000 people in 132 countries found that the key element of what many people consider happiness – positive feelings – is much more strongly affected by factors other than money, such as feeling respected, being in control of your life, and having friends and family to rely on in times of trouble. This study is the first international study to differentiate between overall life satisfaction and day-to-day emotions.

Day-to-day positive feelings depend on a lot of other things, besides money. The results showed that money can make you feel better in a limited way. But positive feelings like enjoyment and laughing can do a whole lot more for people. They can help people grow and learn and become a more resilient, better version of themselves.[17]

The big factors in determining happiness levels are satisfaction with your job and social relationships. How much pleasure people get from their job is independent from how much it pays. Job satisfaction is important, but relationships are most important. Having close family and friends, making progress toward important goals and values, and being involved in work one enjoys continue to be strong predictors of happiness. While making money can give people more comfortable lives, it won't necessarily contribute to life's pleasant moments that come from engaging with people and activities, rather than from material goods and luxuries.

To increase happiness, people need to spend time with loved ones and pursue life experiences that make them feel good. Life satisfaction isn't about buying material goods or investing money to create more money...it's about spending time with people, doing interesting, fun, and challenging activities. Though financial health can make people happy, what really matters in difficult times is support from other people, humor, and praying. Money helps, but it can't soothe all of life's problems. Money can buy happiness, but it may not sustain long-term life satisfaction.[18]

THOUGHT-PROVOKING QUESTION:

When I was deciding whether or not to have a child, I always thought it would be too expensive to raise a child. I saw all the equipment, Clothes, and toys that my friends and family bought for their children and thought I'd rather spend my money on travel and education. Then a good friend asked me a question that put this financial consideration in perspective. This question helped me to determine if money was really the issue or if I was using it as an excuse or a distraction from another underlying issue. She had me ask myself this question:

QUESTION:

"If you had $2 million in the bank and no financial concerns, would you consider having a child?"

For me, I realized that money wasn't the issue, because I still didn't want to have a child even if I had this amount of money in the bank. This helped me become aware that there was probably another issue causing me to pause and hesitate about having a child. Whatever your answer, asking yourself this question shows you how much money plays in your decision-making process.

3. HEALTH & BODY:

Am I healthy enough to have a child and how will having a child affect my body?

When I spoke to women about deciding whether or not to have a child, many expressed concerns about how their bodies would be affected. Some, as I mentioned in Step 1, expressed signs of tokophobia, telling me that the concept of pregnancy and childbirth was disgusting to them. Others were concerned about their fertility and whether or not they would be able to have children since they've heard so much conflicting information about peak fertility years, yet thought it seemed that there were an increasing number of older women having children. Women were concerned with how their bodies may be affected during pregnancy, childbirth, and post-partum. Although many of these women were still deciding whether or not they wanted to have children, they were concerned about gaining weight, not being able to lose weight after pregnancy, or how their "boobs" would look afterwards, especially if they breastfed. Many didn't want to be "fat" afterwards.

Although we have more information than ever in our world about health and medicine, there still seems to be a gap in knowledge among women when it comes to our bodies and pregnancy, childbirth, and taking care of ourselves after childbirth. It's almost as if this information is given out on an "as needed" basis, when a woman does get pregnant. Some women aren't really interested in this type of information until they are ready to have a child. There are others who are put off by what they've been told or heard from friends and relatives about the physiological process of having a child. Many of us go through high school, into college, and then into the workforce, and unless we study nursing, medicine, or some other health-related profession, we may not have the opportunity to learn about the intricacies of what really happens to women's bodies when they become pregnant and give birth—unless we have friends or family who share their experiences with us.

Several years ago, I went to a book signing in Arizona when Naomi Wolf launched her book, *Misconceptions: Truth, Lies and the Unexpected, on the Journey to Motherhood*, in which she explains how the medical community makes childbirth and becoming a new mother more difficult and suggests more natural approaches to make the experience more enjoyable. There were about 50 people in the bookstore to hear Ms. Wolf. Many were young women in their mid to late twenties. About fifteen minutes into her speech, Ms. Wolf paused and looked into the audience. She said she stopped because she got the feeling that some people in the audience didn't seem to know what she was talking about. She asked the audience directly, "How many of you don't know what an episiotomy is?" More than half the women in attendance raised their hands. She explained that an episiotomy is a procedure during childbirth where the doctor may have to make an incision in the perineum area – that are between the vaginal opening and the anus – to help the baby's head pass through. It is sutured up afterwards. There were very loud groans and moans from the audience.

In this section, I address some of the major concerns that women mentioned to me during my interviews. I do this to help these women get informed and hopefully alleviate any misinformation and reduce fears. With more information, you can have a better sense of control and make a better decision for yourself. What I have definitely learned when it comes to having a child – everyone is different and you have to do what's right for you.

1. Tokophobia revisted

In Step 1, I mentioned that some women suffer from tokophobia, or the fear of pregnancy and/or giving birth. I mention it again here, because if women have an adverse reaction to pregnancy or childbirth, they may think that this means they do not want children. Their fear may be tainting an underlying desire that they aren't able to discover or articulate until after they recognize and acknowledge their fear.

I believe that I suffered from tokophobia. I really could not fathom the thought of being pregnant and giving birth, although I witnessed the birth of a friend's child and births on Discovery Channel. For women who may think that they may have tokophobia, I want to provide some reassurance that there are ways to cope and overcome your fears. In my case, I knew that I didn't want to give birth vaginally. I had interviewed women who had problems with their episiotomies – nerve damage, incontinence, and some after multiple births who had to have their pelvic floor reconstructed. Although some medical professional and organizations refute that these conditions are common.

I was also influenced by my husband and his constitution. He is not one to deal well with blood or me being in pain. He is a sensitive person, and I've been present where he's almost passed out when seeing other people's blood. I've also seen him tormented and worried when I am hurt or in pain. I thought that if I had to go through hours of labor, he may be traumatized.

That is why I decided on an elective c-section or what is also called, "Preplanned" and "Patient Choice" c-sections. This decision is not popular in the United States, with only about 267,340 elective c-sections being performed from 2001-2003.[1] And some medical organizations and personnel say that elective c-sections are unnecessary. In 2005, when I was

115

pregnant in Arizona, it took me many OB/GYN visits and interviews to find a doctor who would give me what I wanted. I brought books and studies to show the doctor that I understood the c-section process and the risks, and to explain why I wanted one.

I also showed him the position of the American College of Obstetrics and Gynecologist's Committee on Ethics which shows that a doctor can ethically give a woman a c-section if she requests one:

"If the physician believes that cesarean delivery promotes the overall health and welfare of the woman and her fetus more than vaginal birth, he or she is ethically justified in performing a cesarean delivery. Similarly, if the physician believes that performing a cesarean delivery would be detrimental to the overall health and welfare of the woman and her fetus, he or she is ethically obliged to refrain from performing the surgery."[2]

I remember the doctor putting me at ease after I told him he was the 6th doctor I had visited, by telling me that very few women come in and ask for an elective c-section. He shared with me that people who request c-sections are clearly in the minority. He told me it was time to stop worrying and to enjoy the rest of my pregnancy. We then determined a date to do the c-section and discussed plans if I happened to go into labor early.

I understand my situation and my view may not be suitable for everyone. The purpose of mentioning it is to help women who are just learning that they may have this condition and that there are options if they really want to have children.

In Britain, the medical community has devised a process for women with tokophobia to help them deal with their fears of pregnancy and childbirth. After a few counseling sessions, if they are still uncomfortable with vaginal delivery, they can have an elective c-section. And, studies in Britain show that women with tokophobia tend to request more elective c-sections.

Take some time to get clear about whether pregnancy and childbirth are issues for you and may be interfering with your decision about having children. Remember there are ways to alleviate and deal with these fears.

2. Age and Fertility

For some women that I interviewed, understanding how age affected their fertility played an important role in their decision. Some said they wanted to make a decision before they were 30-years-old because they felt it would be more difficult to get pregnant after that point. Others set their cut-off date at 35 or 40-years-old.

The following statistics explain the possibility of having children and miscarriages by age:
- At age 30, 75% will get pregnant within one year, and 91% within 4 years.
- At age 35, 66% will get pregnant within one year, and 84% within four years.
- At age 40, 44% will get pregnant within one year, and 64% within four years[3]

Miscarriage rates by age:
- Between 20-24 years old: 9% of pregnancies end in miscarriage.
- At 35-years-old: 20% of pregnancies end in miscarriage.
- At 42-years old: 50% of pregnancies end in miscarriages.[4]

117

The trend is toward "older" moms

Although women know that they are more fertile when they are younger, there is a trend for women to have children when they are older. As mentioned in the *Having a Child is a Choice* section earlier in this book, most women are having children in their late twenties. There have also been predictions that because people are living longer and are taking better care of themselves, it's becoming more possible to have children when women are older. There is a paradigm shift going on about age and having children. If people can live to be 80 or 90 these days and we have children in our late to early 40s, we will only be 58 to 60 when they graduate from high school. Sixty-years-old doesn't seem as old as it has in the past.

Some claim that women in her 40s have some advantages. Due to perimenopausal hormone fluxes, she's more likely to release more than one egg each cycle, upping her chances for fertilization. Also, because she's more financially sound, she's better equipped to pay for medical treatments, such as artificial insemination or invitro fertilization, if they are deemed necessary. There is a chance of chromosomal problems (Down syndrome rate is now 1 in 100 and by 45, it may be as high as 1 in 30). And the chance of a pregnancy ending in miscarriage for older mothers is about 40%. [5]

Studies have also shown that people who wait until they are older to have children are happier than people when they are younger. According to a study of 200,000 people from over 86 countries, people over the age of 40 who have children are happier than those over 40 without children. Men and women under 30-year-old with children are less happy than those under 30 who are childfree.[6]

The same study showed that having more children makes older parents even happier. For parents over 50, each additional child increased the likelihood the adult would report feeling happy. Multiple kids make the 20-something set miserable. For most parents under 30, those with 2 children appeared unhappier than those with one child. Likewise, single-child parents tended to be unhappier than adults with no children.[7]

Age and fertility affect both men and women's ability to conceive a child. Don't let fear of not being able to have a child force you into a decision that you aren't ready to make. Everyone is different. But there are many more options and assistance in becoming pregnant or having children. More people are waiting and having children later in life.

3. What happens when you get pregnant

When I spoke to women about having children, some could not wait to be pregnant. They were excited and hopeful. Others felt the opposite and were uncertain whether they could handle it. The reality is that everyone's pregnancy is different. Everyone has an experience unique unto themselves, even though may share the same side effects. And, the same woman can have different experiences with each pregnancy.

According to Christine, a mother of 5, "With my first pregnancy I did not know what to expect. I had horrible morning sickness and sometimes would be laying on the bathroom floor at work - I know this sounds disgusting - because the cool tile was soothing to me." She went on to tell me that her other pregnancies were all different. She didn't have morning sickness with all of them. With another, she was tired, and another she retained a lot of water and looked very bloated.

For me—the woman who was afraid of pregnancy—my pregnancy was easy and uneventful. I had no morning sickness, was more tired than usually in the beginning, and felt elated. We have a photo of me about four months pregnant that was taken during a Thanksgiving party where my skin is glowing and I do look radiant. It's one of my favorite photos.

So the bottom line about pregnancy is that you aren't going to know what you are going to feel like until you actually do it. The trick is to keep an open mind and get help with any uncomfortable side effects. And, remember it's only about 37 to 42 weeks.

Changes in the brain

When it comes to the changes a woman's body goes through when pregnant and having a child, some women are concerned about becoming a different person and they won't be able to function like they used to. Some have heard stories of "mommy brain" forgetfulness and not being able to remember names and directions, as well as "What was I going to say" situations. Women need to know that their brains do change when they are pregnant and continue to do so after they have a child. While a woman's body grows a child within her, her brain is being rewired, as well. And while she cares for her child, her brain is being rewired as she does tasks and activities that she hasn't done before.

In Katherine Ellison's book, *"The Mommy Brain: How Motherhood Makes Us Smarter,* she says that new mothers become afraid when they don't function like they used to right after having a baby, but that "this is often not a product of harm that motherhood does but sleep deprivation, stress, or the impact of having to learn so much new information in short amount of time."

In her book, Ellison explains the research of Dr. Kelly Lambert, who studies rodents to learn how pregnancy affects mother's brains. When a whole new person is developing inside you, your brain changes. There are some mild compromises, such as memory impairment, when your brain is trying to function to carry divergent activities – your normal tasks that you are already used to and familiar with, and the creation of a new life, which is a new experience and is causing you to live your life differently. The end result is that your brain develops new connections, as your body naturally changes due to the pregnancy and you learn new activities in association to the pregnancy and new motherhood.

Dr. Lambert's tests showed how brains of rodents changed after they had pups. Her new mother rodents performed better in tests for spacial memory which caused them to learn mazes more quickly, and they maintained spacial and cognitive ability in old age. The rodents that were exposed to their young had an enhanced rate of neurogensis – the production of neurons in the brain. This occurred early in postpartum when maternal behavior was being established. When pups got older and ventured away, less neurogensis was observed. The mother rodents also had a reduced stress levels throughout their lifetime.

"The changes that occur during pregnancy show the plasticity of the female brain," says Dr. Kinsley. "In rodents, hormonal events of single and multiple pregnancies and lactations appear to rework the female brain in way that facilitate learning, memory, problem solving, stress reduction, and life-long cognitive activities. Rat studies are relevant to humans because the parts of a rat's brain that activate during maternal behavior are almost identical to those in a human female."

The plasticity of the brain through the influence of hormones, mental stimulation, and repetitive behavior, as with mothers in pregnancy and child rearing, contributes to the changing and growing of the brain over a lifetime. New neurons and connections are made all the time. There are times in life when there are windows of brain development—when the brain is more plastic than at other times. Motherhood is one of those times.

When a woman is pregnant, her brain is changing due to hormones and neurochemicals as her body create a life. Her sense of smell becomes sharper, and her sensitivity to other's emotions is heightened which allows her to become more focused on her offspring and their cues. She becomes more efficient at recognizing the emotions on the face of others, especially fear, disgust and anger.

Work of Ruth Feldman of Bar-Ilan University and her colleagues in 2007 showed a correlation between levels of oxytocin (the love and bonding hormone, which is also associated with the formation of breast milk) during pregnancy and the amount of time that mothers and infants spend gazing at one another.

Hormones help mothers defend their infants and prepare them to be loving mothers after giving birth. But, hormones have a downside that can cause some new mothers to suffer from depression. After delivering a baby, there is a sudden drop in rich concentration of hormones that exist during pregnancy. Some doctors suggest that this acute pull back may play a role in the severity of postpartum depression.

Your body will change, but you won't know how being pregnant will affect you until you get pregnant. Everyone is different. A woman's pregnancy is unique to her, even though there are common experiences that pregnant women may share. Your brain and body will transform so that you can grow a baby, deliver a baby, and care for a baby after birth, which can have some beneficial effects.

4. Other concerns about health and body

The women who still were deciding whether or not to have children shared with me their major concerns about their bodies and health when it comes to having children. These were giving birth, breast feeding, post partum depression, and weight gain and loss. Before they make their decision, they wanted to have some idea of how all these situations would impact their bodies and lives. They wanted to figure out if they could handle these situations. They had heard stories and witnessed what friends and family went through and weren't quite sure if they could or wanted to.

Birth options

"My delivery was in a bath tub, in water. I wanted to have a home birth. I wanted to be very aware and present during the birth... I didn't want to be drugged up. So I did a lot of preparation, I did yoga and meditation, so I managed to have a very tranquil birth at home. It didn't hurt in the slightest.
"The whole time my mind was focused in each contraction on the thought 'my baby is closer to coming out. It wasn't like 'this is so painful.' So I transformed that intense feeling into a hope of seeing him."
-Super model Gisele Bundchen told a Brazillian TV Channel about the birth of her first child.

There are so many options in giving birth these days. You can give birth vaginally, with or without medication. You can be induced and give birth vaginally. But, if that doesn't work out, they can give you an emergency c-section. Or you can get an elective c-section. If you had a c-section the first time, you

123

can have another or have a VBAC (vaginal birth after c-section). And, you can have a baby in a hospital, in a birthing center, at home, in your bed, in a bathtub or holding onto a poll (yes, I actually know someone who held a pole, squatted and delivered a baby). It all depends on your insurance, your doctor, and what you are willing to pay for yourself.

Since women do have many more options and there is more competition for mothers, some hospital maternity wards are being redone to make it more family friendly and relaxing for new mothers. The hospital I gave birth in had all private rooms; it felt more hotel-like than hospital-like and offered in-room spa services.

In the United States, 71.5% of births are vaginally delivered vs. 29.5% through C-section.[8] Here are the pros and cons of vaginal versus c-sections since these are the two most popular approaches.

The pros of vaginal births. You can have no pain relief or pain relief. That is your choice. The baby is born when it's ready—not before. Birthing through the birth canal stimulates your baby's lungs, preparing its body to breathe. The mother can also hold her baby the moment it's born, and if no anesthetic is in the mother's system, her baby will be able to see, hear, smell and taste its mother. Let's not forget the sense of achievement that the mother (or both parents, for that matter) feel when they've labored and delivered their baby. It allows the parents to share the experience of childbirth, with the father often actively coaching and supporting the mother. When all is done, the parents are left with a sense of empathy for what the baby has endured during the birthing process, which can be bonding.[9]

The negatives of vaginal delivery. For starters, labor is very painful, and any fear the mother feels can alter her hormonal states. Pelvic floor dysfunction can appear at time of birth or later – they arise when coughing, sneezing, laughing, or crying and involve leaking urine, gases, or feces. Of a population of 4,000 women in the United States, 80% had given birth, 25% reported anal incontinence and 15% reported stress urinary incontinence. Over 20% of the deliveries were induced. 14% of the women had an episiotomy. Other negatives include potential tears in the vagina or perineum, side effects from anesthesia or epidurals, nerve damage to the baby, and tiredness—labor will take as long as it takes—this can be exhausting. After prolonged labor, if an emergency c-section is called for, it is more difficult to recover from this type of c-section. Some women also find the invasion of privacy from constant vaginal exams to be a negative aspect of vaginal delivery. [10]

The pros of having a C-section are: The mother will be fully conscious, and she will know more about how the birth will proceed. C-sections offer an avoidance of labor, which is important for those fearful of childbirth. Elective C-section avoids all the uncertainty and pain of typical labor. C-sections also offer protection of the mother's pelvic floor – reducing the risk of stress incontinence by stretching these muscles. Damage is minimal and temporary with a horizontal incision, leaving a barely visible bikini line scar. And unlike vaginal deliveries, there is no damage which would likely affect your sex life.[11]

The negative aspects of a C-section include: Physical discomfort after surgery, potential weakening of the abdominal muscles, sudden heavy bleeding during the procedure (you will lose about twice as much blood during a C-section than during vaginal birth). Babies born via C-sections before the 39th week may have a higher risk of serious lung and breathing problems. That is why most C-sections are scheduled at 39 weeks and beyond. As with any other procedure, there is a risk of infection, but antibiotics are administered to limit the possibility. The costs of vaginal birth and C-sections in hospitals are very similar in the U.S.[12] Mothers who have C-sections also incur weeks of forced inactivity post-partum. In addition, the rate of breastfeeding is lower after a C-section.[13]

Another approach to consider is hypno-birthing, where women learn self-hypnosis to help them have natural birth with no drugs, no screaming. and little pain. But, in reality pain-free and painless births are not really promised. But this approach can help a women relax so the birth process is more comfortable. Their deep relaxation practice and utilization of empowering terminology – surge instead of contraction—can help women have a better birth experience.

One reason why a good birth experience is important is that if a woman has a positive experience, it is more likely she will bond with her baby. It has been shown that women who experience difficult labors have a difficult time bonding with their babies.[14] So, it's important for women to learn about their options and feel comfortable with pursuing whichever approach they think will work best for them.

The best thing to remember when you are contemplating having a child is to know your options, know who you are, and what you think you can handle. Giving birth is not a competition. Just because one woman gives birth one way, that doesn't mean you will be more or a woman or stronger if you give birth another way. Remember, the end goal of the birth process is to safely deliver a baby. And it's nice for it to be a good experience for the parents, as well. Be honest with yourself and what you can do. There are many women who are confident and comfortable with what their bodies can handle. I wasn't one of them, and I enjoyed my elective c-section. Luckily, there are many options and you need to find a doctor who will work with you, if you choose to have a child.

Breastfeeding – pros and cons

Although women hear that "breast is best," the women I interviewed were a bit concerned about breastfeeding – not sure if they could do it or want to do it. It made them question the whole "baby" question. Once again, it's hard to say what you are going to do until you have a child, but I've seen women who wanted desperately to breastfeed and couldn't and women who thought they wouldn't who did. I've heard women talk through their tears about their guilt for not being able to breastfeed. They feel badly about themselves as mothers.

When I had my child, I decided from the start that I wouldn't breast feed. I spoke to friends and family and realized that having a child was enough for me to cope with, considering my lack of experience and knowledge about babies and all things maternal. I felt good about my decision for the most part, until strangers I met at social functions tried to make me feel guilty. As I mentioned my concern to a friend, she told me that she breastfed her baby, and her child ended up getting cancer, so she said not to worry about it. Her experience and insight put breast feeding in perspective for me, and made me feel better about my decision. There are many factors that can influence a child's health and development. Breastfeeding is only one of them.

So what are the benefits of breastfeeding? Early breast milk that comes first contains colostrum which is very rich in nutrients and antibodies. Then the early milk changes to mature milk which contains fat, sugar, and protein and provides antibodies, as well. Breast milk is easier to digest for most babies than formula, which is made from proteins from cow's milk. Breast milk is said to fight disease and protect babies from illness. Some mothers also told me that breastfeeding was more convenient, that they could feed and soothe their babies wherever they were. They felt it was easier than preparing a bottle, although some mothers pumped so that their spouses could help in the feeding, as well.

Breastfeeding after birth also seems to have lasting health benefits on mothers – reducing the chance of having cancer, diabetes, and cardiovascular disease. Also, breastfeeding releases oxytocin during nursing. This helps women become more relaxed. The body gets in the habit of releasing this hormone the more you breastfeed. This can help alleviate stress later in life.[15]

The downside of breastfeeding is that it's not easy for everyone. It's not a skill that comes naturally for some women, and they may need help to learn how. And, breastfeeding does not guarantee that your child will not get sick. I know of many breastfed children who get allergies, ear infections, and colds. There have also been reports questioning the quality of breast milk, and that some mother's milk may contain toxins due to the environment they live in and the food they eat. Also, if a woman returns to work, she's going to have to learn how to pump at work.

Returning to work is why some studies claim that many women don't continue breastfeeding for a year, which many people consider is ideal. In 2005, about 75% of women started breastfeeding at birth. By six months, only 42% still were. [16] Mothers who stayed at home three months or longer were about twice as likely to breastfeed beyond three months.[17]

Knowing what I know now, and being healthier now than I was when I had my child, I would try to breastfeed. Although I did feed my son formula, he had had no major health issues, no allergies, no ear infections, and he only got a cold maybe once or twice a year. I think I'm more comfortable being a mother now, so that breastfeeding doesn't seem so foreign, overwhelming, or scary.

Postpartum Depression

Women I spoke to were very concerned about the possibility of suffering from post-partum depression. They said they've seen and known friends that have struggled with post-partum depression, which made them worried about having a child, The U.S. Center for Disease Control reported in its 2008 PRAMS research that about 15% of all postpartum women in the U.S. suffer from postpartum depression. That is more than the women who are diagnosed with breast cancer, 205,000 (national Cancer Institute), or suffer from stroke (300,000). Other studies report prevalence rates among women from 5% to 25%, but methodological differences among the studies make the actual prevalence rate unclear. And, women aren't the only ones that can experience post-partum issues. Among new fathers, the incidence of postpartum depression has been estimated to be between 1.2% and 25.5%.[18]

According to the Mayo Clinic women can suffer from two categories of post-partum emotional complications. The baby blues, which lasts only a few days or weeks, may include: Mood swings, anxiety, sadness, irritability, crying, decreased concentration, and trouble sleeping. Postpartum depression may appear to be the baby blues at first — but the signs and symptoms are more intense and longer lasting, eventually interfering with a mother's ability to care for her baby and handle other daily tasks. Postpartum depression symptoms may include: Loss of appetite, insomnia, intense, irritability and anger, overwhelming fatigue, loss of interest in sex, lack of joy in life, feelings of shame, guilt or inadequacy, severe mood swing, difficulty bonding with the baby, withdrawal from family and friends, and thoughts of harming yourself or the baby.[19]

Post-partum depression can be caused or influenced by physiological reactions in the body after giving birth or due to the emotional adjustments during early motherhood. After giving birth, hormonal changes in a woman's body may trigger symptoms of depression. During pregnancy, the amount of two female hormones, estrogen and progesterone, in a woman's body increases greatly. In the first 24 hours after childbirth, the amount of these hormones rapidly drops back down to their normal non-pregnant levels. Researchers think the fast change in hormone levels may lead to depression, just as smaller changes in hormones can affect a woman's moods before she gets her menstrual period.

Or, levels of thyroid hormones may also drop after giving birth. Low thyroid levels can cause symptoms of depression, including depressed mood, decreased interest in things, irritability, fatigue, difficulty concentrating, sleep problems, and weight gain. A simple blood test can tell if this condition is causing a woman's depression.

Other factors that may contribute to postpartum depression are more situational and can have an emotional impact, including:

- Feeling tired after delivery, broken sleep patterns, and not enough rest often keeps a new mother from regaining her full strength for weeks.

- Feeling overwhelmed with a new, or another, baby to take care of and doubting your ability to be a good mother.

- Feeling stress from changes in work and home routines. Sometimes, women think they have to be "super mom" or perfect, which is not realistic and can add stress.

- Having feelings of loss—loss of identity of who you are, or were, before having the baby, loss of control, loss of your pre-pregnancy figure, and feeling less attractive.

- Having less free time and less control over time. Having to stay home indoors for longer periods of time and having less time to spend with your partner and loved ones.

Through my experience, I've learned that women and new mothers don't get the support and help they need, especially after having a child. Many women have moved away from extended families to pursue education, careers, and relationships in different cities. They may have focused so much on their careers and don't have much knowledge of information about how to take care of themselves or a child after they have a child. Although I had some very nice friends who helped me and my husband during those first few months, I sometimes wondered, "Where's my village?" as I remembered the title of Hillary Clinton's book, *It Takes a Village,* about how we as a society are needed to help raise the next generation of children. For the most part, I felt I had to figure everything out on my own. I didn't have any class or single resource I would turn to that could help me structure my new life. I had to rebuild it piece by piece and it took quite a bit of time, energy and effort to recreate it. And, because my husband had a good job and I decided to stay at home, I could take the time to figure out how to incorporate this new role as "mother" into my life. But, others aren't in the same situation.

I also don't think our society acknowledges what a life changing and altering experience it is to have a child. We just assume that because millions of babies are born every year, that it's a part of life and because women have been doing it for so long, we just expect them to get on with life after they give birth. But modern life is complex, and women have multiple roles and responsibilities that now compete for time and energy with their roles as mothers. So, I think there'd be less post-partum depression if we were nicer and more supportive of women and mothers in general. Of course, I don't have any data to back that up, but it just makes sense.

New mothers can suffer from different degrees of postpartum depression. But there are ways to alleviate the symptoms and ultimately recover. Physical activity, diet, the support of friends and family, and medicine can help one cope. If this is one of your concerns in making your decision to have a child, know that there are resources and support to help. Contact Postpartum International Support at www.postpartum.net for more information and. read Brook Shield's book, *Down Came the Rain: My Journey Through Post-Partum Depression*, to hear how she overcame debilitating post-partum depression.

Weight

Weight isn't a concern reserved only for women who are deciding whether to have a child. We have a fixation about weight in the United States. I guess that's for a good reason since according to the US Center for Disease Control and Prevention, about one-third of U.S. adults (33.8%) are obese.[20]

The guidelines for pregnancy weight gain are issued by the Institute of Medicine (IOM), most recently in May 2009. Here are the most current recommendations:

If your pre-pregnancy weight was in the healthy range for your height, you should gain between 25 and 35 pounds, gaining 1 to 5 pounds in the first trimester and about 1 pound per week for the rest of your pregnancy for the optimal growth of your baby. If you were underweight for your height at conception, you should gain 28 to 40 pounds. If you were overweight for your height, you should gain 15 to 25 pounds. If you were obese, you should gain between 11 and 20 pounds.

Having a baby does not mean you have to be fat. Lots of new moms regain their pre-pregnancy figure within 8 to 12 months. True, it takes time for your body to get back to normal, but it will if you eat properly, get active, and let nature do the rest.

I wasn't in the best shape before I had my child. It wasn't until after I had him that I started eating better and taking better care of myself. I learned that to be healthy, you need to make your health a priority. So even if you are still deciding whether or not to have a child, you can still start taking care of yourself.

One problem I noticed when I was home with my son, is that my life slowed down, and I spent much more time inside the house with him. When there isn't much to do, it's easy to eat. And, when your child gets older and starts eating solid foods, it's easy to just clean off their plate by eating their left-overs. These little behaviors can add up.

A University of Minnesota study showed that moms and dads of young children tend to exercise less, eat more junk food, and weigh more, compared to kid-free men and women. The study looked at 1,500 relatively young adults and found that parents, particularly the moms, ate more fattening and sugary foods, including drinking soda. They also exercised less than their childless counterparts. This is a high-risk time period for gaining weight. For some women, that's because they are bored taking care of kids, so they do less and eat more. On the other hand, others gained weight because they have so much to do that they grab high-calorie fast food, rather than cooking.

Try not to worry about every detail

During my interviews, I noticed that women worried and got distracted by "what-if" scenarios. When deciding whether or not to have a child, it's best to understand what happens to your body, but also realize that everyone and everyone's pregnancy and birth experience will be different. Recognizing that you have concerns about your body and health is a great first step in learning and understanding how to deal with and handle the situation if it arises. It also gives you a chance to prepare and plan. If you feel that your worries are more severe, you may want to talk to an expert to help you overcome them. Also, many of the concerns with child birth, breastfeeding, post-partum depression, and post-partum weight issues are really short experiences that a person goes through and then moves on. You won't be doing these things again unless you decide to have more children. Many women have wonderful pregnancies and deliveries and then move on to care for their child.

Why having support is important

Having help and support is key to dealing with many of these health issues. If you are deciding to have a baby and are concerned about pregnancy and giving birth, I find the more help you have during and afterwards, the better. Being independent and self-sufficient is a quality we stress and admire in the United States. Asking for and receiving help, even when we desperately need it, causes some women to feel like they are somehow inadequate and not good mothers. Being pregnant and having a child is not something that should be done alone. The more help and support you get, the easier and more enjoyable your experience will be.

THOUGHT-PROVOKING QUESTION:

One evening as my husband and I were lying in bed and I was reading yet another book on pregnancy and how a woman's body changes when she gets pregnant, my husband matter-of-factly asked me, "If I could get pregnant and give birth, would you have a child?" It didn't take me long when I said, "Yes, I think I could do it." I was surprised that I said "Yes," so quickly. Apparently, I had issues with the physical part of being pregnant and giving birth.

QUESTION:

If your significant other could get pregnant and give birth (even if he is male – just use your imagination), would you be more likely to have a child? Or, if you knew that you could have a child and not have to go through the physical aspects, would you want to have a child?

4. SIGNIFICANT OTHER:

What's Your Partner's Opinion?

What do you need to know about men and what do they need to know about themselves in order to make your decision to have a child? In this section, I share want I learned about men and their thoughts about having children. If you aren't in a relationship, how can you decide whether you want to have a child on your own?

Men think that women have an "upper hand" when deciding to have a child

When I spoke to men, most implied and explained that women had an "upper hand" in making the decision to have a child. Because men don't get pregnant, give birth, or primarily care for children, they felt that a woman or their wife really had the final "say" in whether they'd have a child.

Although men can have their own preferences about whether they want a child or not, they have to find someone to go along with their desire. The reality is that men can't have a child by themselves unless they adopt or hire a surrogate. One man explained that deciding to have a child isn't really a "dilemma" for men "Because we don't get pregnant and give birth. Having a child affects women more. It's hard to force a woman to have your child. "

I noticed this line of thinking during my interviews. Men acknowledged that women, because of their biology, naturally have to bear more of the responsibility for having a child. Because of this physical reality, men will defer to their wife or significant other to see if they want to have a child or not before making their own decision.

A man may have an opinion about what they want, but it comes down to whether the woman wants to have a child or not. As one husband said to me, "If I want a child and my wife doesn't, then that's it. I'm going to respect her opinion. I'm not going to force her to have my child." Or as another man said, "If my wife didn't want children, I wouldn't be with her." When I interviewed other couples and asked them if they wanted to have children, the man would usually say, "Well, it's up to her." Or, "If she wants to." Or, "Let's ask her."

Other men acknowledged women's "upper hand" in deciding to have a child, by expressing their fear of being "trapped" in a relationship because of an accidental pregnancy. "If a woman decides she wants to have a child with me and she goes off birth control, even though she told me she was on it, and she gets pregnant, I don't see how I made a decision to have a child. I made a decision to have sex with her, not to have a child. She made the decision to have the child."

For years I would ask my husband, "Do YOU want to have a child?" And he'd ask me right back, "Do YOU want to have a child?" I wanted to know his thoughts, and he wanted me to make the decision because having a child would affect my life more.

So, when women are trying to make their decision to have a child and they are in a relationship, and her significant other may seem ambivalent or confused, he may be waiting to see what her preference is. What's important for men to remember is that it is their decision, too. They need to take some time to honestly assess what they want in their life. A man may go along and have a child because their wife, girlfriend, or significant other wants one and it will make her happy, but he hasn't considered if he really wants to be a father. That is the question a man needs to ask himself: Do I want to be a father?

There's a difference between being a sperm donor and being a father. Women need to remember this, as well.

What do men think about having children?

Studies show that most men want to have children. According to research, almost 87% of males aged 15 to 44 who have no children say that they want to have children at some point in their lives. Among childless men between the ages of 40 and 44, a narrow majority (51%) still want children.[1]

The same study showed that most men don't think they need children to be happy. Only 8% of *childfree* men believed that a person needs children to be happy. And only 14% of *fathers* agree that children are necessary to be happy.[2]

Most say that being a father today is harder today than it was generations ago. Of all male adults, 57% say it's more difficult to be a father today than it was 20to 30 years ago. Among dads, 63% say the job is harder now.[3]

How many men have children? Surveys show that in the United States, 20% of men have fathered one child, 25% fathered two, and 33% have fathered 3 or more children. And, 22% of men between the ages of 40 and 44-years-old had not fathered any children. [4]

In my interviews, I heard men voice the same preferences and concerns that women had when making a decision to have a child. They could also be classified into categories. There were men who were family-oriented and knew they wanted to have children. They felt having a family was a huge part of having a fulfilling life. Then there were others who were completely against the idea of having a child, and they wanted to focus on their careers, making money, enjoying their freedom, and travelling. Or they didn't think they had a good family or father role model and thought it best not to have children, they didn't know how to relate to kids and didn't want to spend time learning how to, and some admitted they just didn't like kids. I also interviewed men who told me that they didn't want kids until they met their wife – that their relationship made them want to settle down and start a family. And, there were men who were undecided.

Marriage isn't just for having children

Times are changing. More people don't think marriage is mandatory when it comes to having children. In a recent study, 70% of Americans disagreed with the statement: "The main purpose of marriage is having children."[5] Other research shows that 38% of Americans say that marriage is becoming obsolete. This is up from 28% in 1978.[6] Another study reveals that 25% of adults aged 18 to 29 who are unmarried and have no children say they are not sure they would want to get married. Another 5% say they are positive they never want to get married.

Even if people don't think you have to get married to have children, lots of people are still getting married. Over 70% of men and women aged 25 to 44 in the United States have ever been married: 71% men and 79% women. The probability that men will marry by age 40 is 81%, and for women, it is 86%.[7]

People are waiting longer to get married. The age of first marriages have climbed since the 1960s, when men got married at 23 and women at 20. Now men are waiting until they are 28, and women are holding off until they are 26.

People still want to have children. Studies show that 74% of unmarried and childless millennials (those born 1982 to 2000), say they want to have children, while 19% say they are not sure and 7% say they don't want children.[8]

140

According to the U.S. Census, married couples represent only 48% of the households. That's down from 52% in the last Census. The reason could be that the fast-growing older population is more likely to be divorced or widowed later in life, and 20-somethings are putting off their nuptials for longer stretches. People in their 20s are postponing marriages for money. An aging population is living alone. Fears of not being able to hang onto a job, more opportunities for women in the labor market, and a shift away from having kids at a young age have proved to be a disincentive for people in their 20s and 30s to join the married ranks.

Men's fertility and biological clock

Women aren't the only ones whose age affects their potential to have children. Male age is associated with a decline in semen volume, sperm mobility, and sperm morphology. Sperm count declines with age. Men aged 50 to 80 years old produce sperm at an average rate of 75% compared with men 20 to 50 years old.[9] Studies have shown that there is an increase in the chance of birth defects due to older sperm.

The age that women have their first child in the United States is about 25, however, that is due to a high number of teenage pregnancies. If those pregnancies aren't taken into consideration, then the average age of first-time pregnancies is 28 years old. In developed countries around the world, the average age for women to have their first child is between 28 and 30 years old. Thirty seems to be an unspoken age where many women think they'd like to have children. At that age, they think they won't have fertility issues, will be young enough to take care of a child, and will have had enough time to pursue their own interests and establish a career (if that's the path they want). Another time limit for women seems to be 40. At 40-years-old, women become concerned that fertility will be an issue and think it's their final chance to have a child. And surveys show that there has been an increase in births for women in the 40 to 44 age group.

But what about men? Do they have some internal time limit –their own internal, "clock" that influences them to start families? They may think not. And, I'm not sure if there haven any research has been conducted to investigate this idea. But from some of the patterns I recognized through my interviews, I think men do have a time limit that inspires them to settle down and have a family. That unspoken and maybe even unacknowledged age is around 40-years-old, give or take a few years.

Randall was an Ivy League educated attorney who practiced real estate law, in the mid-Atlantic region, and he was very straight-forward in his plan. He said he wasn't even going to consider having children until after he was 40-years-old because he wanted his freedom and wanted to establish himself in his career. He thought by 40, he'd start looking for a "wife," preferably in her late 20s to early 30s who wanted a family. Randall told me that at 40 he'd still have energy to be with his kids and that he'd be more established career-wise so that he had more flexibility in his work schedule.

After Randall told me his plan, I started hearing from others about their brothers or other relatives and male friends who never wanted to be married and avoided the topic of children until they turned 40.

An acquaintance told me of a brother who was 42-years-old when he married a woman about 10 years younger than himself. "It was as if he felt he was at the 'right time' in his life. He spent his younger years doing what he wanted and was established in his career as an engineer. He was more stable." She explained, after he turned 40, it was if he made it a priority to meet someone. Within two years, he was married, and a year later, he had his first child.

A real estate investor I spoke to told me he got married when he was forty years old to a woman who was 29-years-old. They were married for 6 years before they had their first child. He is now 49-years-old and told me that he thought waiting until he was older was a good decision because he was established in his profession. He told me he had a decent bank account, a few beautiful houses, and his own business that gave him flexibility to be with his child. He said he tries to take better care of his health so that he can have energy to play and interact with his child. But, he's very happy he waited.

Unlike women, age doesn't seem to be that much of a factor for men. We hear of the more famous men in society having children when they are older. Here is a list of men who had children in their later years: Former British Prime Minister Tony Blair (45), Mick Jagger (57), Phil Collins (51), Rupert Murdoch (72), Michael Douglas (58), Rod Stewart (60), "Beatle" Paul McCartney (61), Charlie Chaplin (73), Anthony Quinn (81), Pablo Picasso (68), Luciano Pavarotti (twins at 67), Larry King (65 and 66), Warren Beatty (62) and Jack Nicholson (53).

Men's concerns

My interviews with men about their decisions to have children were revealing in that they didn't have as many concerns about having children. The most common concerns men had were:

1. Finances: Can I afford a child?
2. Time: Do I have time to be a parent?
3. Career: How will having a child affect my job?

4. Sex, I mean Relationship: How will my relationship be affected? (Will we still have fun, and sex?)

Can I afford a child?

Although I discussed finances previously, men have other concerns besides how much it will cost to have a child. For some men, the ability to provide for their family is important to them. Even though, as a society, women have made advances in the workplace, men still think and feel they need and want to be the provider. In one study, when asked **hypothetically** about the idea of a spouse out-earning them, 73% of women said they were comfortable with their husbands earning more and only 59% of men said they were comfortable with their wives earning more. But, when women were **actually** the breadwinners, the comfort level shifted for both men and women, and 87% of women said they wouldn't mind their husband's bringing in more income than they do. And only 42% of men said they were okay with their wife earning more than they do.[10] Yet, as of 2008, almost 26% of women in dual-earner couples earned at least 10% more than their husband or spouse. [11]

Men were also concerned about whether they could retire if they had children. They wondered if the cost of having children would make it more difficult to retire. One male executive recruiter for a search firm told me, "I have 3 kids. I'm never going to retire." It has been shown that people who don't have kids can and do retire early.

Another man shared his philosophy about money and children and why he decided to have a family. He said he's done pretty well financially, but material possessions weren't satisfying for him. He said he'd rather spend his money on his family. He said it didn't make sense to him to work hard and make money just to buy things or give it to the government or a charity. He said he doesn't understand people who want to work all their lives and then die with all this money in the bank. "What's the purpose of that? At least I know the money I made is being invested in my children and their lives and futures. I'd rather invest in them.

The state of the economy has a direct impact on men's thoughts and feelings about having children. If men don't feel good about the economy or their financial future, they tend to get more vasectomies. Each year, approximately 500,000 men choose vasectomy as a permanent birth control method.[12] The actual numbers are not known because most are done in private clinics. According to a CNN interview with the Cleveland Clinic about their vasectomy statistics, the clinic said that after the financial collapse in 2008, vasectomies at their clinic increased by 50%. [13] Men were saying that they were going to lose their jobs and health insurance and wanted to have a vasectomy. They realize they don't have the long-term financial security in the current financial environment, and they didn't want to have any more children. It's more difficult to raise children in an uncertain future. At the Cornell Institute for Reproductive Medicine in New York, they saw a 48% increase of vasectomy consultations during the economic downturn of 2008, compared with the prior year.[14]

Time

Men that I spoke to about having children were aware that having a child meant that they had to spend time with them. But they weren't sure if they had enough time to do so. One single man said he barely had time to work and see his girlfriend and couldn't imagine how he'd fit in time to be with a child if he had one. He said he works quite a bit and wouldn't know where he'd be able to cut back to fit a child in.

Studies show that in 1965, married fathers with children under 18-years-old living in their household spent an average of 2.6 hours per week caring for those children. In, 1975, that rose to 2.7 hours per week. In 1985, it rose to 3 hours per week. And, from 1985 to 2000 the amount of time father spent with their children doubled to 6.5 hours in 2000.[15]

I'm not presenting this information to validate that this is the proper amount of time fathers should spend with their kids. Studies have shown it's not necessarily the quantity of time, it is the quality. If you participate in an activity with your child where you are interested, engaged, and connected, that means more to the child than the amount of time.

Job/Career

Men are concerned that when they have a child and may have to spend time away from work, they will be perceived as less serious or committed. But, recent research shows that working men who take time out for their children are perceived positively, whereas women are perceived in a negative light.

In an interview regarding his book, *The New Dad: Exploring Fatherhood within A Career Context*, Brad Harringon a professor at Boston College, says that research has shown that women are seen as less committed to their jobs after they have children. For men, the opposite happens. Men are seen as more competent, committed, and promotable.[16] However, men aren't likely to take advantage of any parental leave time or flex-time.

Relationship and Sex

I address this concern in the Section 9 - Relationships: How do your relationships with our partner, family, friends, employer, and co-workers affect your decision to have a child?

Women who decide to have children by themselves

If there is no significant other in your life, but you are still contemplating having a child, realize that you would be part of a growing trend. More single women are having children on their own. The trend and public opinion is that marriage isn't a reason to have kids. In 1997, single moms delivered 32% of the 3.9 million live births in the US.[17] Ten percent were to teenagers, and 17% to single moms between 20 and 29 years old. Today, one-third of all American children are being raised in single-parent homes, with more than 80% of them being headed by the mother.[18] That means there are about 25 million children in the United States living in single-parent homes.

In Mikki Morrissette's book, *Choosing Single Motherhood: The thinking woman's guide*, she explains that single women contemplate the same issues as partnered women when thinking about becoming a mother. The main difference is for single women to acknowledge the lack of a backup parent that can provide some support and an emotional balance for the child and yourself. Other considerations are: believing you can handle having and raising a child on your own, acknowledging you want to fulfill your own personal need, realizing you may miss your freedom, understanding that it's okay to have a child without a partner but you may have to include people to fulfill those needs, you have enough financial resources, and to get over believing that you have to be perfect as a mother.

One main concern that women have when thinking about having a child on their own is whether the child will be okay having just one parent. Parents contemplating divorce who may get full-custody of their children, wonder the same thing. According to a study conducted by Cornell University in 2004, being a single mother does not appear to have a negative effect on the behavior or educational performance on children. The study followed almost 1,500 6 to 7-year-old children from multiethnic families starting in 1997 until they turned 12 and 13 years old in 2004. The researchers wanted to see how single parenting by mothers affected children as they developed.

The researchers learned that a mother's education and ability level were more important than the family income and quality of the home environment. There were no negative effects, regardless of how long the children lived with a single parent during the previous six years. [19]

The women who I spoke to who were contemplating single motherhood said that having children was part of their identity and that they couldn't imagine their lives without being a mother. They feel compelled to have a child and start a family on their own, and will do so if they haven't met the right person.

Ashely, a 25-year-old hair stylist, told me very confidently that she wants to have children some day. She told me that having a child is something she has always wanted in her life. She can't imagine her life any other way. She said that she wouldn't date anyone that isn't interested in having a child. She also said that if she is not in a serious relationship that holds the possibility of a child in the future by the time she is 35 years old, she will have a child on her own. She doesn't feel there is any stigma to having a child by herself.

Delia, a 23-year-old speech therapist, told me she also wants to have children. She said that she loves children and wants to have the experience of loving and nurturing her child. She also said she's not going to think too much about it for a few years while she works to establish herself in her career and take some time for herself. She says that she wants to travel and date. And, although it goes against her more traditional family values, she says she would consider having a child on her own if she wasn't married by the time she was 37 years old. Delia explained that having a child is so much part of how she defines herself, that it's an experience she wouldn't forgo just because there wasn't a man or husband in her life.

Both of these young women come from families where the parents have been married for over 30 years, they have siblings, and the mothers worked. These women made it clear to me that that having a child is what they want in their lives, and they are willing to make it happen, whether they had a partner or not.

QUESTION:

For those with a significant other: If your significant other or partner happened to die suddenly, would you regret that you didn't have a child with them or would you be content to know that at least you had the opportunity to share their time and experiences with them while they were here?

For those without a significant other: Answer the question at the end of the "Regret" section.

---

5. EMOTIONAL:

Am I Mature Enough and Ready to be a Parent?

Some people that I interviewed wondered if they were emotionally mature enough or emotionally ready to have a child. Most often, these were younger people who were either in high school or college or had recently graduated from college. Older people who questioned their maturity wondered if they had the emotional disposition to interact with or handle a child on a daily basis. Even some men in their mid-30s claimed whole-heartedly that they were not mature enough to have a child. (At least they were honest).

Human brain matures at about 25 years of age

As I mentioned in an earlier section, the human brain is said to mature around the age of 25. Over the past several years, scientists have used magnetic resonance imaging (MRI) technology to study the way the brain develops from childhood to adulthood. What they've learned is that the brain develops in stages – the back part maturing first and the front part maturing last. That back part, which matures first, controls sensory functions such as vision, hearing, touch and spatial processing. The next area to mature coordinates those functions so, for example, you can find a light switch in the dark. And the last part is the prefrontal cortex, which handles the executive function of the brain, which includes planning, setting priorities, organizing thoughts, suppressing impulses, and the ability to weigh consequences of one's actions. Scientists now claim that the bad decisions that teenagers sometimes make are due to their still-developing brains. Since higher level brain functioning is considered to develop at the age of 25, one would wonder if waiting to have a child until this age is more beneficial to all parties involved.

One study conducted at Dartmouth College showed that 18-year-old brains are different from of those brains of 20-year-olds. Researchers scanned brains of 18-year-olds going away to a college at least 100 miles away, and compared them to older adults. The scans showed significant changes in the freshman brains in the regions of the brain where emotions and thoughts are integrated. The researchers claimed that brain changes were due to environmental demands that the subjects were exposed to. Yet, even with these brain changes, the teenage brains were still different and not as developed as an adult brain.[1]

An early book written to help people decide to have children, which was published in 1978 (before MRI scanning research), actually suggested that people wait until they were at least 25-years-old before having a child. The authors said that waiting until 25 increases the chance that the decision a person is making is truly their own. The authors also explained that their research showed that people who waited until after 25 to have their first child were more satisfied as parents than those who had a child earlier. Part of their reasoning was that the longer a person waits, the more life experience they have and the more ready they will be. [2]

Although there are no hard and fast rules about when someone is emotionally ready or mature enough to have a child, this research does provide a scientific guideline to consider. At least I know that I will be sharing this information with my son when he is old enough.

Clean up any alcohol or drug addictions and get a grip on mental or emotional issues

If you have drug or alcohol addictions, mental illness, are in a violent or hostile relationship, you are not in a good emotional state or situation to have a child. Get help first. I say this because I interviewed several people who came from families where alcohol or drugs were a problem or they had a parent who suffered from a mental illness. They all said they wished their parents cleaned up their act before they had them. Some even wished their parents didn't have children at all.

These children of addicts and alcoholics suffer tremendously. Some said they decided they wouldn't have children because they didn't want to risk hurting a child of their own. Although many were resilient and formed good lives for themselves, they said they didn't have a good role model and didn't know if they would be able to handle the stresses of parenthood. They said they know what it feels like to be hurt as a child, and they didn't want to inflict that kind of emotional pain onto another human being. Unfortunately parents who suffer from these diseases may not be in the best state to realize their situation or that they have a problem. They are caught up in their experience, without realizing how it is affecting their lives or the lives of those around them.

One daughter of a heroin addict that I interviewed said that her childhood was hell and she raised herself and her brothers and sisters. Her grandparents helped and were somewhat of a support, but they were busy trying to handle their daughter – her mother. She ended up becoming a lawyer and doesn't drink, smoke, or take drugs. She is religious and doesn't want to have children. She told me that she helped raise her siblings and that was enough.

There are also a plethora of studies that show how alcoholism and other drug addictions have serious and derogatory consequences for children who are born to and live with parents who are afflicted with these diseases. Currently, it is predicted that there are more than 28 million American children of alcoholics and 11 million are under 18-years-old.

Studies show that the detrimental effects of being born to an addicted parent are:

1. The children have a higher risk of becoming addicts themselves.

2. There is a strong genetic component for the onset of early alcoholism in males, where sons of addicted fathers have more of a likelihood to become addicts themselves. If parents take drugs, their children are more likely to, as well.

3. The family experiences increased family conflict; emotional or physical violence; decreased family cohesion; decreased family organization; increased family isolation; increased family stress, including work problems, illness, marital strain, and financial problems; and frequent family moves.

4. Addicted parents often lack the ability to provide structure or discipline in family life, but simultaneously expect their children to be competent at a wide variety of tasks earlier than do non-substance-abusing parents.[3]

Children deserve a fair start. So, if you are contemplating having them and you have an issue with drugs, alcohol, or violence, it would be best to focus on yourself and get help first.

What does "emotionally mature" mean?

There are different ways to define emotional maturity. As it relates to having children, here are a few guidelines. You are emotionally mature if you have experienced the following:

1. You do not rely on your parents and other relatives for basic financial and emotional support, and have achieved a certain level of independence. You can pay your own bills and are financially able to raise a child?

2. Since achieving autonomy from your family, you have identified and found a job, schooling, exploration and pursuit of a talent worth developing. You have reached a certain level of stability or level of satisfaction in a profession, passion, or vocational pursuit, and you know how to cope with failure within this endeavor. Surviving a major setback is a maturing experience. Have you had the chance to try something and fail and learn how to recover? Have you accomplished things you wanted to? Reached educational goals? Professional goals? You don't have to have arrived at the final destination, but have a good idea of where you want to go. Or you've developed a certain level of confidence so that you feel that you can handle the ups and downs of life.

3. You have learned to live intimately with a significant other. You know how to share intimate space, adapt to another's schedule, needs, and priorities. You have learned how to develop tolerances of differences of habit and preferences.

4. You like and respect yourself and have confidence in your own choices, opinions, and judgments. You are secure in self, for the most part.

5. You having a pretty clear idea of the direction you are

155

going in life and have short and long-term goals.

6. You have established a strong relationship bond with your significant other. Are you both able to communicate your needs, listen to each other, and ask for help when necessary?

7. You believe you can handle and cope with change reasonably well.

8. You realize you can create your life by understanding how you were influenced by your past. You understand where you've come from and have an idea of what you want in life.

QUESTION:

Pick a friend or family member you like and admire that has children and that you think is a good parent. Write down the aspects of their life and qualities that they have that make them emotionally mature to have and raise their children. Sometimes looking at someone else helps us identify and articulate those qualities that make a person mature enough to have a child. Now compare yourself to the list you just created. Do you have those qualities?

Or, ask a friend whose opinion you trust to tell you honestly if they think you are ready to have a child. Then, ask them to tell you why or why not.

---

6. PARENTING:

Do I Know How to Take Care of a Child and Do I Want to?

Engaging in a parenting role is one of the major responsibilities of having a child. When I spoke to people who were deciding to have a child, some of them couldn't wait for the experience and opportunity to raise a child. Others were hesitant due to the enormity of being responsible for another person. Others weren't interested at all.

I am still amazed that I was allowed to leave the hospital with a baby and yet I had no training or experience in how to care for him. We spend so much time and energy learning a trade or profession so that we can make a living, yet when it comes to taking care of a child, we just assume it comes naturally. There are doctors, nurses, teachers, and therapists who, due to their professional training, have more experience and knowledge than laypeople, and can fortunately apply their experience when they have their own children. Most of us settle for doing what we think is best.

How do I know if parenting is something I want and can do?

When people think about whether or not they want to have a child, one of the first things they consider are their feelings about children. Although this is a reasonable place to start, it's not always the best indicator.

People make the assumption that if you enjoy being around children, it is indicative that you should have a child and become a parent. If you don't like being around kids, you shouldn't have children. As I explained in the maternal instinct section, this isn't necessarily accurate. People who love kids do decide not to have them, and people who never liked kids end up loving their kids and becoming fabulous parents. The "if you like kids become a parent" litmus test doesn't always hold up. Of course, these internal preferences can be clues to our interests and desires and shouldn't be ignored, but they are not conclusive. The only exception is if you know you have a very strong desire not to have children, then don't have them.

Also, the enjoyment of children should be kept in perspective, since they are children only for so long. Childhood is a process that consists of different stages of development that human beings go through to reach adulthood. They start out as babies, grow to toddlers, tweens, teenagers, and adults. They aren't babies or toddlers or teenagers forever. When considering the lifespan of a person, some of these stages are relatively short. Babies start sitting up at six months and may even start crawling. They are constantly growing and changing. Children turn into adults, which they are for a longer period of time – the rest of their lives really. So when you think about being a parent, realize that for the most part, you will have a longer relationship with them as adults than children.

Understanding that raising children involves going through multiple phases may help potential parents realize that being perfect at each phase is unrealistic. I interviewed people who shared that the "baby" phase was easiest for them. Others said that they liked their kids until they got to be 15 and then really didn't know how to communicate. Others shared that they didn't relate well when their children were younger, but as adults, have rebuilt their relationships. Others spent much of their time ensuring that their children had good, stable childhoods, but have a difficult time connecting and relating to them as adults. One thing to keep in mind is that raising a child, like any relationship, is about connection. Being open and willing to learn how to relate to our children is always an option for us, at whatever stage they are in. It may not be easy, but it can be done.

The stay-at-home mother of nine children and wife of a professor told me that her husband really doesn't do well with young children. He is more of an intellectual and doesn't have the patience to take care of or deal with young children. Before they had children, they agreed to their arrangement, where she would do all of the care taking when their children were babies and toddlers. The father would become more involved when they were older, around 7 or 8 years old. Before anyone starts to judge them, it's not like he didn't hold or talk to his children when they were babies. He just didn't do a lot of the daily feeding, changing of diapers, or bathing. But, it worked for them.

Also, by realizing that childhood consists of phases of development, you may want to ask yourself if you have any preconceived notions about how children act or behave that may be influencing your decision. Some people I spoke to think all babies have colic and that children are just "blobs." They may have a negative perception without realizing that children can also have positive attributes, like the way they smile when they see your face or how their eyes light up when they see something new.

One example of preconceived notions of how children act is that many people think that adolescence is always, or almost always, a time of psychological turmoil. Some experts believe that top psychologists have fueled the perception that the teenage years are usually times of high family drama and that adolescence has to be a time of stress, tension, rebellion, dependency, conflicts, peer-group conformity, etc.[1] But it has been shown that the public is routinely exposed to a biased sampling of teenagers—to those teenagers that do have problems.

Most studies indicate that only about 20% of adolescents undergo pronounced turmoil, with the substantial majority experiencing generally positive moods and harmonious relationships with their parents[2] Furthermore, marked emotional upset and parental conflict are limited largely to adolescents with clear cut psychological problems, like depression or conduct disorder, as well as adolescents who come from disrupted family backgrounds. So the claim that adolescent angst is either typical or inevitable doesn't hold up. To the contrary, it is the exception, not the rule.

Also, cross-cultural data shows that adolescence is a time of relative peace and calm in many traditional and non-Western societies. For example, in Japan and China, the teenage years usually pass without incident. There is evidence that the Westernization in these areas is associated with increasing adolescent distress.[3]

So, given your views and opinions of children and childhood, it may be a good idea to consider whether you can handle the care-taking phases of development, but you may want to approach your decision from the perspective of whether or not you want to have a long-term relationship with another person. After all, they will be adults longer than children. And your relationship will grow and change as they grow and change throughout life.

Parenting does matter. It's not all about genes.

There have been many studies that claim that a child's genetic predisposition is what determines a child's behavior and outcome. Genes control who they are, and parenting is not as important. This makes many parents relieved and takes some pressure off. In Bryan Caplan's book, *Selfish Reasons to*

Have More Kids: Why Being a Great Parent is Less Work and More Fun Than You Think, he describes different studies that show genetics are more of a determining factor in raising kids than parental involvement. He advises that since a child's future is largely up to them because of their genes, and parents need to be happy, too, that parents should relax and enjoy their kids more, instead of trying to be the perfect parent.[4] However, Caplan points out that in low income families, parenting is more important than genetics. An impoverished environment can have a negative impact on a person's development.

Genetic studies have looked at family parenting style, parental diet, secular orientation, marital status, divorce, and remarriage to determine if these shared family experiences have any effect on a child's personality. And the research says they don't.[5] They have no effect on the adult personality. However, researchers have said that these studies are conducted on a wide range of families that are fairly functional. A dramatically violent or abusive childhood can leave lasting effects.

When studies have shown that children from divorced families divorce, or that people who were hit as children turn out more violent, or that depressed children had a mother that was depressed, those who support the genetic theory of personality and behavior claim that children grew up this way, not because of their environment, but because the kids have inherited these tendencies from their parents.

However, other researchers disagree and say that a child's personality and outcome is not solely determined by their genetic disposition. They claim that the way a child is nurtured and their interaction with their environment—parents, friends, and other social influences—influences how their genetic nature is expressed. There is a big difference between saying a child's personality is ***determined*** by their genes, rather than *influenced* by their genes. Psychologists say that parents do have the ability to influence a child's personality, interests, character, intelligence, attitudes, and values. Parents can influence a child's likes and dislikes and how they behave at home, at school, and with friends. A parent can influence whether their child is kind and considerate or mean or selfish. It may take some effort on the parent's part to deal with a child's genetic nature, but it can be done, such as when a parent recognizes that this child has an aggressive nature. But, instead of ignoring it and let the child fend for himself, the parent can help channel that energy into a productive outlet, so that the child may end up developing into, for example, an exceptional hockey player.[6] These researcher believe that the ultimate manifestation of a child's temperament depends on how a child is raised, taking into consideration the genetic disposition that the child is born with.

So, what do kids need for a healthy development?

When I first started on my journey to determine if I wanted a child, I realized that I didn't know much about babies or children. I was curious to know what they were like to see if I could handle one, especially since I was operating from a deficit. So, I bought a few books about child development to give me a better understanding. The famous wire-monkey studies were mentioned in several books and seemed to provide the foundation of early childhood care. That study affirmed that babies and children needed affection and love, and they suffer traumatic results if they don't get any.

These studies took place in the early 1950s and were conducted by Harry Harlow a professor at the University of Wisconsin who started breeding monkeys to conduct experiments. When the baby monkeys were born, they were taken away from their mothers, put in cages, and fed. They had no contact with other monkeys and lived in total isolation. As a result, they would maniacally rock back and forth in their metal cages, sucking on their thumbs till they bled. When they encountered other monkeys, they would shriek in fear, run to the corners of their cages and stare at the floor. If they felt threatened, they would lash out in vicious acts of violence.

They fought each other, were vicious to their own children, and would sometimes kill them. Most psychopath monkey mothers just perpetuated the cycle of cruelty. When their babies tried to cuddle, they would push them away. The confused infants would try again and again, but to no avail. It was as if their mothers felt nothing. Because of their early deprivation, these monkeys had to be in isolation for the rest of their lives.

Harlow realized these young monkeys needed more than proper nutrition. He decided to raise the next generation of monkeys with two different pretend mothers. One mother was formed out of wire mesh; the other was made out of soft terrycloth. Instead of hand-feeding the babies, he put their milk bottles in the hands of the wire mothers. What was important: food or affection? No matter what mother held the milk, the babies always preferred the cloth mothers. They spent more than 18 hours a day nuzzling with their soft parent. They were with the wire mothers only long enough to eat.

Through these observations, Harlow asserted that primate babies are born with an intense need for affection. They cuddled with the cloth mothers because they wanted to experience the warmth and tenderness of a real mother. Even more than food, these babies craved the feeling of affection. Harlow wrote that, "It's as if the animals are programmed to seek out love."

When the need for love wasn't met with the wire monkeys, the babies suffered from a tragic list of side effects. The brain was permanently damaged so that they didn't know how to deal with others, sympathize with strangers, or behave in a socially acceptable manner. As Harlow would write later: "If monkeys have taught us anything, it's that you've got to learn how to love, before you learn how to live."

Other studies were conducted on the effects of isolation and maltreatment of orphans in Romania in the 1960s. The brain activity of these children was examined, and it was shown that there was reduced activity in the amygdale and pre-frontal cortex regions that are essential for emotional and social interaction. These orphans couldn't perceive emotions in others and couldn't interpret facial expressions. They had low levels of hormones important for social attachments. And these hormone deficiencies persisted for years afterwards. Researchers concluded that because of their isolation and neglect, these children didn't get "educated' in feeling. They had no one to care for them to show them how.

What does it take to be a good parent?

When I interviewed people about their decision to have a child, many wondered what it took to be a good parent. There are so many approaches and suggestions that it's easy to get confused about what's really important. They wanted to know if they had what it would take to be a parent and if they were capable.

My research showed that it was important to be a mindful parent, rather than a reactive one, and that more you practice at parenting, the more instinctive it becomes. Also, children learn more by watching you than by what you tell them. And, there's nothing wrong with getting advice when you aren't quite sure what to do. There are very few "natural" parents.

Ellen Gallinksy, the President of the Families and Work Institute, interviewed children and parents and came up with these eight important parenting skills; [7]

1. Capable of making a child feel important and loved
2. Able to respond to the child's cues and clues
3. Accept the child for who he or she is
4. Promoting strong values
5. Using constructive discipline
6. Provide routine and rituals
7. Being involved in a child's education
8. Being there for a child (children judge a parent on whether or not they are "there for me")

The following is another list of good parenting principles by Laurence Steinberg, Ph.D.[8]

1. What you do matters. Be a mindful parent. Your children learn by watching you.

2. You cannot be too loving. Children suffer because parents are too busy, too selfish, or too preoccupied, but it's not possible to spoil a child with love.

3. Be involved in your child's life. Be engaged with them and develop an interest in something they like.

4. Adapt your parenting to fit your child. Your child is unique; adjust your parenting according to your child's temperament and through developmental transitions.

5. Establish rules and set limits. Be firm and fair, learn how to handle conflicts over rules and how to relax them when they get older.

6. Help foster your child's independence

7. Be consistent

8. Avoid hard discipline

9. Explain your rules and decisions
10. Treat your child with respect

There have also been several books over the years that discuss the pitfalls of extreme parenting, but they really focus on mothering. Some describe these ambitious mothers as former career women who now want to apply their same level of professionalism and perfectionism to parenting. Or they are moms whose sole focus is the betterment of their children so they focus almost all of their time and energy on their children. They schedule their children in a multitude of programs – soccer, tennis, ballet, horseback riding, art – to help their kids develop interests and skills and to keep them busy. ("It's better than sitting in front of a TV," one mother told me.) All of this scheduling and keeping up with other moms has lead to a trend of burn out and dissatisfaction with motherhood.

To counter this trend, books are now coming out about how to be a more relaxed parent in order to enjoy children more. In *Good Enough is the New Perfect* by Becky Gillespie & Hollee Temple, they explained the trend of intense parenting and how to scale back to enjoy parenting, including taking less demanding jobs that fit your lifestyle and create the life that's good for you and your family, rather than comparing yourself to others.

What's important to kids?

There was one major study that asked children their thoughts about how their parents parented. What was interesting was that kids didn't give higher scores to their parents because they spent more time with them. Instead, the study showed that a child's perception of their family's economic health was strongly linked to how they rate their parent's parenting skills. Children gave their fathers higher grades when they saw their families as economically healthy and their fathers were employed, and the father was living at home with them. Children give nonresident fathers lower marks. The same was true for mothers. Children who viewed their families as less economically healthy and had money problems gave their mothers lower grades.[9] The only times when the families' economic health did not make a difference was in a parent's encouragement of family routines and traditions, and in the father's involvement in what is happening to their children in school.

Several decades of research show that parents in families who are struggling to survive economically are less able to focus on their children and less able to be warm and responsive.[10] Studies also show that many, but not all, otherwise healthy children born into poverty do less well as they grow older and that these changes are "related to adverse living conditions, not inherent factors and traits within the child. Also, friends and communities they live in play and important factor in how children develop.

QUESTION:

How would you evaluate the way you were parented? What didn't you like? What did your parents do well? If your (fictional) child asked you to explain to them why you decided to have them, what would you tell them?

7. CAREER:

How Will My Professional Life Change or Do I Want to Stay at Home?

I'm not sure that I ever could have or would have run for the Senate, or for President, or had the job I currently have when my daughter was young. I think I would have been so conflicted and torn apart every trip I made, every weekend I missed. But I was lucky that I always worked; I always had that balance. I have had a lot of wonderful jobs. But my public career really came after Chelsea was grown.
-Hillary Clinton Interview in *Working Women* magazine

When I spoke to people who were contemplating whether or not to have children, both men and women were concerned about how their career or job would be affected, and how their job would affect their potential children. They wondered whether their current job could cover expenses and provide for a comfortable lifestyle. Women in particular were wondering how a child would affect their job and their future employment potential and opportunities. They also wondered how being at work and not with their child would affect their child emotionally, behaviorally, and developmentally. These undecided potential parents had witnessed family and friends cope with the tenuous balance of work and family and weren't sure if they could handle it.

Some of the specific concerns from the women I spoke to were: In a world where it takes two incomes to survive these days, what if I want to quit my job and stay at home to be with my child? Will I be considered a bad mother if I want to return to work? How will my employer and co-workers view me – will

I still be taken seriously or viewed just as a "mommy"? If I return to work can we afford childcare?

Because work and career have become central aspects of a woman's life – for personal fulfillment, talent expression, self-esteem and financial purposes – it's only natural that one would consider how having a child may impact this aspect of her life. Once you have a child, the way you live and work will be different and modifications will be made. These can be minor or major changes, depending on how you want to restructure your life, and will depend upon your passions and interests, the job you have and how it relates to your identify and finances, and your feelings after you have your child.

Deciding whether to work or stay-at-home may not happen until after you actually have your child

It's difficult to try and guess what your life will be like after you have a child until you actually do have a child. Some women think before they have a child that they will continue working, and then discover six months later that they'd rather work part-time or stay at home. Then there are those women who think they want to stay at home and realize they are better moms and people if they return to work. Your decision about your work will be unique unto you and be affected by the combination of influences.

In a *Wall Street Journal* interview with Sallie Krawcheck, a president of global wealth and investment management at Bank of America, she shares what prompted her to return to work. She said that when she was pregnant with her son, she thought she'd do some part-time non-profit work. But after she had him, she said "A few months in, I found myself on my hands and knees trying to teach him to crawl. And, then there was another day when some friends went to play doubles tennis, and it upset me that I wasn't included. Those two things happened, I said, 'I cannot do this to my family. It's not fair to them, and I need to work. I just got too much energy to do that to that poor kid. Let me do that to our clients. Let me do it to the folks that are paid to work with me. I have too much of that neurotic energy. So I really have never questioned whether it's right for me and for my family to work."

And how she dealt with guilt:

"When you leave and the three-year-old is crying, 'Don't go Mommy, don't go,' you have to have a heart of stone not to feel guilt. But I never showed fear. I had a certainty that I loved what I was doing. It was good for my family. And so I was pretty steady about it." [1]

Here are some women who shared their stories with me.

Marcia graduated top of her class in law school and was the editor of *Law Review*. Right after law school, she got a great position at one of the top law schools in Washington D.C. She worked there for five years and had a great reputation and was considered to be on partner track. During that time, she met and started dating a criminal defense attorney who had his own practice. They married and a few years later had a son. Marca's mom helped watch their boy, and Marcia went back to work. Two years later, Marcia had another son. But, there were some medical issues that required Maria to be at the hospital. Her firm wasn't flexible for her, even though she put in years of stellar performance. She felt like she had no choice but to leave. She spent the next two years making sure her son's health was stable and then obtained a position as a legal writing instructor. She told me that never anticipated not working in a firm environment or not working at all for a time. But she feels her job gives her the flexibility she needs while her sons are young.

Beth, a marketing executive in Georgia, returned to work after having her first child. Her mother, who lived nearby, watched her daughter while she went back to work. Beth did this for a year and then quit. She told me that it pained her to see her daughter go to her mother whenever he needed to be soothed, wanted to interact, or was hungry. She said she didn't feel like the mom and was an observer to her child's life. Beth, who was always very career-minded and professional, told me that she was shocked that she felt this urge to stay home. Up until that point, her entire life was geared toward developing a career. When she had her child, she didn't know how to incorporate mothering into her life. She really felt as if she had no choice but to quit. Beth had another daughter two years later, and then returned to work after her youngest turned eight.

Isabelle was a real estate attorney in Florida. She told me she returned to work after her maternity leave and felt good about her childcare situation. Her parents moved to Florida specifically to help her and her husband care for her daughter. But, every morning on her drive to work, Isabelle found herself crying all the way there. After three months of tearful commutes, she felt it was an indication that she needed to be at home. She tells me she misses her work, but she feels that she needs to be home with her daughter for the time being. She told me that her soul is now at peace, and she is confident that when her daughter starts school, she will look to return to law.

Helen, an attorney for a small-staffed sporting goods organization, took her maternity leave and returned to work within three months. She and her husband, also an attorney, had family that lived a few hours away, and they hired a matronly nanny to help. Both sets of grandparents would come to visit and would stay to spend time with their grand-daughter. The nanny would sometimes spend the night and helped Helen until her daughter turned ten-years-old. Helen's job also allowed her some flexibility where she could work from home some days. She ended up working for that company for almost 20 years. Helen shared with me that it was difficult at first to leave her daughter with the nanny, but once she realized her daughter was in good hands, she could focus on her work. She also told me that when she came home, she left her work at work and focused on her daughter. She said that practicing corporate law gave her more of a predictable schedule and wasn't as demanding as practicing law at a firm.

Linda is a recruiting manager at a technology company in Seattle, and after her daughter was born, she took a four month maternity leave. She knew that she wanted to return to work because she said she had always been career-oriented and didn't want to stay at home. She felt that her life would become too narrow, and the thought of spending her days with other moms in play groups or driving her kids to activities didn't sound fun to her. She felt that there's really nothing to do at home, and she liked having things to do. When her maternity leave was over, Linda found a good home childcare center that was run by an elderly motherly woman and returned to work. She took another four months off when she had her son a few years later, and returned to work. This time, returning to work was a little more difficult she admitted because her son has a few minor health issues. Linda said she never felt like she missed anything by not staying home. She said she didn't worry about seeing the first step or hearing the first word because when she did see her children take a step or say a word for the first time in her presence, it was the first time for her to see it. Another positive about returning to work she shared was that when she and her husband divorced, she didn't worry about being able to provide for herself.

Then there was, Diane, who worked in marketing for a tech company. She said she planned on staying home with her child and quit her job when she went on her maternity leave. But, after six months of staying at home, she called her former boss and asked to come back. She said she loves her son, but that she felt that she'd be a better mother if she had some mental stimulation and challenge during the day. She said she didn't get that same kind of intellectual challenge at home and really missed it. She was quite joyful with her decision and wasn't at all afraid to admit that she wasn't cut out to stay at home.

Julia, an immunologist, told me that she returned to work full-time after her first child was born. When she had her second child, her first was about to enter kindergarten. She decided to reduce her hours because her son's starting school made her realize that he was growing up and she wanted to spend more time with him. She also wanted to share in the transition he was making and participate in his class. Reducing her hours would also let her spend time with her youngest.

Granted not all women have the luxury to stay at home. In some families, women are sole breadwinners in families or contribute a large portion to a family's finances, which gives their family a less stressful home life. Or, her income allows for luxuries that make her family's life a little sweeter.

Thinking about how having a child will affect your career is not unusual, since so many more women do work. Over the decades, mothers in the United States have been entering the workforce, reaching a high of 59% in 1997 and then dropping to about 52% in 2004. The number of college-educated mothers is even higher, where 71% were working in 1997, but dropping to 63% by 2007.

The percentage of married working mothers:

In 1948, 17%

In 1976, 31%

In 1984, 47%

In 1988, 51%

In 1997, 59%

In 2004, 52%

The percentage of college-educated working mothers:
In 1997, 71%
By 2004, that number dropped by 11% to 60%.
By 2007, 63% .[2]

However, there is a trend that full-time work outside the home is losing some appeal. Maybe the challenge of trying to do it all isn't as alluring as it once seemed previously. A study showed that 62% of employed mothers (with children under 17) wanted to work part-time, up from 48% in 1997. And, only 21% say that full-time work is idea for them, down from 32% in 1997. [3]

With regard to stay-at-home moms, 48% of mothers say that not working outside the home is the ideal situation for them, up from 39% who felt that way in 1997. Only 16% of stay-at-home moms say working outside the home would be ideal for them, down from 24% in 1997. [4]

So when making your decision to have a child, remember if you want to return to work, you won't be alone. There are many working mothers out there. If you decide to stay at home, there are also many women doing that, as well. There are also other mothers who are doing part-time work to keep their professional skills current and earn income, but who still have time for their children.

To make the decision that's best for you, remember it will be important to give yourself time to be with your child and adjust to motherhood. Take advantage of whatever maternity leave you get. Giving yourself room to get used to this new role will help you determine how you want to structure your life with regard to your work and family. You are always free to make adjustments along the way to accommodate your life. About 75% of moms change their job in some fashion after having children.[5] And, it's more common these days for mothers to move in and out of the workforce so that sometimes they are employed and sometimes they are at home. It may not always be easy, but it is doable.

What factors women consider when deciding to work or stay at home

When deciding whether to stay-at-home or work, women consider the following:

1. How much they enjoy their work and how much it means to their identity.

2. The type of work they do and whether they can still perform at the level they are accustomed.

3. The organization they work for and whether they have supportive maternity leave programs or flextime opportunities.

4. How much their salary contributes to the total household income.

5. How much money they make vs. the cost of child care.

6. The emotional factor of being at work rather than caring for their own child.

7. Whether they feel that their child needs them.
8. Which arrangement makes them feel good – working, staying at home or working part-time.

How does work affect children?

One of the main issues deciding working women have when making their decision to have a child is how their work will affect their potential child. They see and hear in the media the mommy war debates about working or staying at home and wonder how having a child will affect their situation. They worry how their future child may be hurt emotionally, behaviorally, or developmentally if they decide to work while their child is young.

Before I had a child, I was very happy that I didn't have to participate in the "mommy wars." I sat on the sidelines and heard friends and family with children discuss the pros and cons of which situation was better. The media likes to play up one side or the other whenever a new study appears, and the results usually cause each group to pause and wonder if what they are doing is "right" for their kids, themselves, and their families. Articles appear all the time about which option is better.

"Child Obesity Linked to Working Mothers."
"Working Moms Have Sicker Kids."
"Working Moms Have Better Adjusted Kids."
"Do Stay-at-Home Moms Set Bad Example for Kids?"
"Daughters of Stay-at-Home Moms Have More Emotional Problems"

These headlines can cause doubt in whichever preference a woman chooses, whether she chooses to work or to stay at home. Neither situation is better than the other. It's difficult to say or prove that one factor—such as work—influences the outcome of a child's development. How a child turns out is based on a variety of genetic, environmental, and social interactions, and really depends on the people and the circumstances of their lives. And what's right for one person or family is not right for another.

But, there is good news. Studies do show that a mother who works and a child being in childcare does not in and of itself affect the bond between the mother and child. Infants are more likely to be securely attached to their mothers when their mothers are **warm & responsive**. Mothers can be warm and responsive if they are employed or not.

What's important is the relationship a mother establishes with her child. When mothers do what they think is right for themselves and their families, their children are more likely to prosper. When the relationship with the mother is lacking, if the mother is less sensitive and responsive, and childcare is of poor quality, the child is at double risk. "High quality" childcare can serve as a compensatory function for a child whose maternal care is lacking.

Studies showed that working did have a negative impact on a child when mothers were not warm and responsive AND when the child experienced one of the following conditions: 1. Poor quality childcare, 2. More than minimal amounts of time in childcare, and 3. More frequent changes in the childcare arrangement.[6]

It has also been shown that maternal employment is good for low-income children. There are many well-documented facts that children who grow up poor, compared with those who don't, are affected developmentally and behaviorally. Quality childcare is more important for children in low-income families. And it is assumed that if a mother is working, she can provide better quality childcare because she is earning money to do so.[7]

That's not all. One study reviewed 50 years of research that compared the children of employed mothers with those of stay-at-home moms. It was found that kids whose moms went back to work before the kids turned 3 had no worse academic or behavioral problems than kids whose moms stayed at home. Maternal employment by itself has very little impact on children.[8] How a mother's working affects children depends on many other factors – the amount of income a mother brings into the family, the mother and father's attitude toward her working, the stresses and satisfactions that parents bring home from their work, and the quality of childcare the children receive. [9]

Another study shows that children whose mothers returned to work within the first 12 months after birth performed worse on a series of cognitive tests when compared to children of stay-at-home moms. But, those setbacks were mitigated when working mothers significantly improved the family income, or selected high quality childcare, or remained sensitive to their children.[10]

Even though it is reassuring to learn that working doesn't have a negative effect on children, there is some research that shows that our society still has biases against working mothers and their children. In one study, an almost unanimous amount of employed parents feel that it's okay for mothers to work if they really need the money. But only half felt that women shouldn't work, if they didn't need to.[11] Yet, in another poll, 75% of Americans reject the idea that women should return to their traditional roles in society and most believe that both husband and wife should contribute to the family income.[12] This goes to show how conflicted we are as a society in our expectations of women and mothers. We think women shouldn't work if they are wealthy enough to stay home, but then believe that a wife should contribute to the family income.

Still, moms who work full-time outside the home are viewed in a negative light compared to moms who don't work. And, more disturbing is that the children of these working mothers were also seen less favorable. Researchers asked undergraduate students who were single and had no children to view a video of a mother and her 4-year-old son playing a game and building a puzzle. They were told that the mother was either a stay-at-home mom, a mom who stayed at home with their child for 18 months and then returned to work part-time, and a mom who returned to work after 2 weeks after having her child and works 40 hours a week. The study showed that the graduate students didn't differentiate between stay-at-home moms and moms who stayed at home and then returned to work. They were fine. However, the students did devalue the mothers employed full-time outside the home. And, more disturbing, the children of the full-time working mothers were seen in a negative light. These children, and their relationship with their mother, were seen as "troubled."[13]

There is nothing wrong with you if you want to stay at home with your child

During my interviews, stay-at-home moms mentioned to me that they felt they were viewed derogatorily because they weren't out in the world doing something "productive." Some felt that others thought that because they were at home they weren't capable of or competent at other work. Some shared scenarios of going to social functions only to be dismissed during conversations once they shared that they were stay-at-home moms - although they had achieved quite a bit of success and were more educated than the people who dismissed them. They shared how they've seen articles in the media that refer to stay-at-home mothers as lazy, depressed, and insensitive to the needs of their children because they are around them all the time. Granted, there are probably people who do have these opinions of stay-at-home moms. I have heard these comments myself. But, as the studies have shown, it appears that working moms unfairly bear the brunt of negative perceptions.

I must confess. I was one of those people who didn't realize what stay-at-home moms did. I had friends who stayed at home, and I respected their decision, but I didn't spend much time wondering how they spent their day. It wasn't until I became one myself that I was enlightened. Isn't that how it usually works? Once you walk in the shoes of another, you really get the sense of what their lives are truly like. By living the life of a stay-at-home mom and spending more time with them, I saw that there were women who truly aspired to be mothers and made their children and family their main priority. They had other interests and talents, as well, but raising a family was one of their core values. I learned to appreciate and respect that everyone has different aptitudes, skills, talents, and interests.

I didn't realize the significance of staying at home until I found myself at home holding my son. Please let me clarify so that I'm not considered an anti-working mother. I'm not saying that staying at home is more important or better than working. For me, I thought that I would return to work – which I did for about six months.

What made my stay-at-home experience significant for me was how I was emotionally transformed by being at home, caring for my son. I was really surprised at how much I enjoyed being with him, even though learning how to nurture and care for him took a conscious effort. My time with him helped me discover that by spending so many years in academia earning degrees and then in corporate and legal environments, I unconsciously turned off my emotions so that I could think rationally, analytically, and strategically, and meet deadlines, and act business-like. I became desensitized to the internal workings for my heart and soul. Caring for my son allowed me to remove the armor that I had built up. Caring for my son forced me to get out of my head and live in the moment. Being with him helped me get in touch with that nurturing and loving side that I had buried.

Now, learning what the life of a stay-at-home mother is like, I have tremendous respect for those who know or decide that this is their path in life. They aren't staying at home as an excuse to avoid the adult responsibility of going out into the workforce. These women did have an affinity and ability to understand and relate to a child's needs. Staying at home with their children allows them to express and apply their talents and skills. I am in awe of these women who have this capacity to connect with children and other people so easily. Their kindness and patience with me was a tremendous help as I was learning how to be a mother. It is unfortunate that these abilities are truly underappreciated and under compensated in our society.

A recent study shows that more women are considering a more traditional lifestyle and are looking for husbands who can support it. A study conducted in London showed that more women are looking to marry wealthy men, with 64% saying that they aspire to find a husband who brings home a larger pay check than they do. None wanted to marry men who earned less. And, 69% said they would prefer to stay at home to look after children if money were not an issue. The report concluded that equal roles in families where husband and wife shared employment, childcare, and housework was "not the ideal sought by most couples." And, 59% said they felt pressured by society to go out to work. [14]

I also interviewed former professional women who became stay-at-home moms after working in the corporate world for many years who found that staying home was more fulfilling than their former business roles. They felt they were making more of a contribution to society by staying at home and raising their children to be good citizens (although working moms do this, too). There were many women who were disenchanted with the corporate environment and policies which they found limiting, stifling, and unfair. They were tired of incompetent bosses and crazy co-workers. Or they felt they weren't appreciated for their work and weren't getting paid enough for what they did. One stay-at-home mom shared that she couldn't fathom going back to the corporate world because being at home taught her how to be in charge of her own life. She shared that going back to work and having someone else dictate her schedule and what she focused her attention on didn't seem appealing anymore. If anything, she said she would rather start her own business.

Planning for work and for children

There are more options today in how you design and structure your life—with or without kids. But when it comes to having kids, there are different approaches to consider in how you can incorporate them into your life. You can pursue your dreams and passions and incorporate children into your life when you are ready. Or, if you know children are a priority in your life, you can select professions and organizations or work at companies that offer work structures and programs that can make having children easier and less stressful. Or some women realize they can't do it all at once and plan to sequence.

The "pursue your passion" approach was described in a speech by Sheryl Sandberg, the COO of Facebook. She encouraged women to go for their dreams and not hold back—to work hard and pursue the risky assignments. She said that investing the time and energy working to create the position you want and enjoy will put you in a better position to carve out the position and lifestyle you want when and if you decide to have a family. She thinks that by paying your dues and advancing to a position of power will give you leverage to add children and family into your life on your own terms. She fears that women who think about a having a family too early in their career may get side-tracked right from the start and will avoid the challenging positions and risky or juicy assignments that are needed to rise to a level of authority that provides the freedom to design the life they want.[15]

A fashion editor of a magazine told me that she pursued her career in fashion first in London, Hong Kong, and now New York City. Then she realized she wanted to have child and through Artificial Insemination conceived a daughter. Because she had reached a point in her career where she was at the top, she had no problem incorporating her daughter into her work life. The child's nanny would bring her to the office throughout the day, where she would visit with her mother and also be entertained by the staff. The editor said she focused on her career and interests, and she felt fulfilled in her work and life.

Another approach to consider, especially if you know that you want to have children someday, is to enter a line of work that is more child-friendly, like teaching, nursing, or pediatrics—really any profession that will give you flexibility with scheduling or time commitments so that you can enjoy your family. In other professions, you may consider pursuing a certain specialty that isn't as demanding—for example, working as a corporate attorney, rather than in a firm, or in academia teaching legal writing. A tech executive told me that she accepted a position with IBM because they have a program where a new mother can take three years off and a position will be available for her upon her return. Other companies may offer flex time, part-time options, or other arrangements that are family-friendly.

Sequencing is another approach to fitting children or a family into your life. Women who realize they can't do it all, especially all at once, plan to have their children at certain times when their careers may not be so demanding or they plan to have children at certain times so they can take time off from work. Some women have planned to get pregnant or have a child while pursing advanced education or other training so they can plan classes around their family life. An attorney took a few years off to spend time with her young children, then returned to school when they entered elementary school. In two years, she earned a Masters in non-profit management, which allowed her to transition and re-enter the workforce in an industry she was more passionate about.

The fact is, some careers are known to require more time and commitment which make it more difficult for women if they want to have children, like neurosurgery and law. About 25% of lawyer moms leave the workplace, compared with 6% of women with medical degrees. The workplace dropout rate for MBA was nearly 30%.[16]

Stay-at-home fathers

One option that some working women are implementing in order to deal with demanding careers is to have their spouse stay home to provide childcare. As of 2007, there were about 165,000 stay-at-home dads, compared to 5.6 million mothers. And in 2009, a record 7.4% of fathers in married-couple families with children under 18 were staying at home with their children, which was a 2% increase from 2008.[17]

For the most part, when mothers stay home, it is usually to take care of family. Whereas, studies have shown that fathers stay home mainly because they can't find a job (51%) or they have been laid off or lost a job (37%). Only 3% said they stay home for childcare responsibilities, and another 3% said that their family didn't want them to work.[18]

But, now, because wives are out-earning husbands, staying home is becoming more of an option. By 2007, almost 25% of wives were bringing home higher paychecks than their husbands.[19] Interestingly enough, according to *Fortune Magazine,* more than one-third of the women who appeared on their 2003 List of Most Powerful Women in Business had husbands who were stay-at-home dads.

When Carly Fiorina was the president of Hewlett-Packard in 2003, her husband, Frank, a former AT&T executive, took an early retirement to help focus his energies on his wife's career. Helena Morrissey, chief executive of Newton Investment Management in London and mother of nine, shared that her husband, a former journalist, agreed to stay home and has since become a Buddhist priest.[20] The CEO of PepsiCo, Indra Nooyi, considered to be the most powerful businesswoman in the world, has help from her husband, who left his job and became a consultant so he could care of their children. And, several female partners at law firms in the United States have stay-at-home spouses who they rely upon for childcare.[21]

The men and women I spoke to who made the decision for the father to stay at home with the child considered the following: who was making the most money, the type of career or position of the other spouse, the personality disposition of each parent, and the cost of potential childcare.

One stay-at-home father I interviewed was a former professional baseball player. His wife was a finance director at a technology company. For several years, the baseball player was on the road and spent a lot of time away from his family. When he decided to retire, he chose to stay at home with their three children so that his wife could focus on her career.

A finance executive told me that her husband was more suitable to stay at home with their little boy because he was a teacher before they got pregnant. He's taken classes in child development and has experience being with and working with kids. Plus, she told me that his teaching salary wouldn't cover childcare, so it only made sense for him to stay at home.

Just as stay at home moms can take advantage of their time to pursue their interests, stay at home dads can, as well. Author Ben Fountain quit work as a lawyer in order to pursue his interest in writing and take care of the children. His wife, who is also a lawyer, kept her job and supported her family financially for years before her husband had any literary success.

Re-entering the workforce

Taking time away from work may be a solution for many families, but experts claim that women who take time off are hurt in many ways. Wages may be lost by taking time off or reducing hours to part-time, having to start at a lower salary when re-entering the workforce, and lost opportunity for promotions. Or they may find that companies may not be interested in hiring them if they took time off because they believe that their skills are stale and are outdated.

I spoke to a few Human Resource Managers to get their perspective. One shared that when looking at people who've taken time off from work – for whatever reason – her company wants to make sure that the candidate can do the job and that they still know how to act and perform in a business environment. She said that sometimes mothers who've taken time off come for interviews and forget business etiquette, how to dress appropriately, and are more lax in the way they handle and carry themselves. But, ultimately, companies really want to know if an applicant has the fundamental skills to do the job.

There are organizations, such as iRelaunch and Momcorps that help women who've taken time off to raise children or care for other family members re-enter the workforce. They help women identify what they want to do next in life, develop an action plan, and provide support, workshops, and networking opportunities to help women obtain the positions they want. They suggest talking and meeting people in the line of work that you are interested in pursuing. Most job offers will probably come from someone you meet through referrals and networking then from blindly sending out resumes.

QUESTION:

This question tries to assess how much your career/job means to you and how flexible you are with taking time off or taking another path. If you got fired from your job right now, how would you feel about it? Is the job something that you are passionate about that you will find another in the same industry? Or are you a bit relieved that you no longer "have to go back to that place?"

---

8. CHILDCARE:

Who Will Help Me?

When contemplating whether or not you want to have a child, remember that childcare is key. Childcare can make having a child so much more pleasurable because then you can have support to work, have time for yourself to rest, especially in the baby stage, and you and your significant other can have alone time. I'm not suggesting this as an opportunity to ditch your child and relinquish all childcare responsibilities. It just helps to have an extra set of hands and some support, even part-time help. Of course, it's even better if it's a family member who wants to spend time with your child because then the child gets time to bond with them, as well. Having help isn't about not wanting to be around your child. It's about being able to take a break to heal, rest, and recharge. Taking care of a child is hard work, and moms deserve to have help if they can find it.

There are different types of childcare options parents have. Of course, the easiest is to have family and friends that are willing to help. But, if not, there are other paid options if you have the budget for it. Some of these options include a night nurse to tend to the baby so you can sleep. There are also other baby nurses that will come to your house and teach you how to take care of your baby. There are nannies that you can find from a service or get from a friend or a mom's network that shares resources. Then depending on if you want to return to work, there are in-home daycare options and external daycare options.

According to 2005 data, 63% or 12.7 million of the 20 million children under 5-years-old were in some type of regular childcare – meaning at least once a week. Those under 5 were more likely to be cared by a relative (41%) than a non-relative (35%), while 11% were cared for by both. Grandparents cared for 23% of preschoolers, 16% were cared for by their father, and 37% had no childcare arrangement. On average, preschoolers spent 32 hours per week in childcare. Children with employed mothers spend on average 16 hours more in childcare compared to children with non-employed mothers.

The most challenging part about childcare is selecting a provider that you trust and is good with your child. When babies are very young, mothers told me they especially wanted someone who was loving, and many preferred older women who ideally had had children themselves. Finding the right person is important and not easy. We hear stories in the media of harmful sitters and nannies, and it's easy to be leery of someone else watching your child. Some mothers are reluctant to share their "bad sitter" experiences because they are afraid of looking like a "bad" mom for selecting the wrong person and possibly putting their child in harm's way. But, what I have learned is that if someone is not right, it's not good to keep them around.

One of the main reasons I decided to stay home from work is that I couldn't find decent childcare for my son—even though I was looking for help part-time. Within six months after I returned to work, I interviewed more than 20 people and tried three. One was an elderly grandmother type who said she didn't need much sleep, but when I came home early, I found her sleeping in a chair while my baby son was crawling around the floor. When she told me about her horrible relationship with her adult daughter and how she tried to cause a miscarriage when this daughter was in-utero, I knew I had to find someone else.

My second try was a mid-twenty Mormon girl who was the eldest of seven siblings. She was only to help out 15 hours a week. But on the second day of her employment with me, after spending just 3 hours with my 5-month-old son, she wanted to drive him to the store so she could register for her bridal shower, left pizza burning in the oven, and constantly chatted with me while I was trying to do my work. Another woman I tried was college educated in child development and worked at a university childcare center for a few years. I thought her background and training made her a great candidate. But, she wouldn't take my son for walks in his stroller, would fall asleep in front of the TV while watching the Food Network, and would volunteer to run errands while I stayed at home with my son. It was clear that working in a childcare facility and working one-on-one in a home environment aren't the same. But, she did my laundry all the time, so my hampers were always bare.

I wasn't alone in my search for good childcare. I talked to friends who tried to hire help and went through the same struggle in finding someone good enough to help with their children. In the end, I was spending more time looking for someone and interviewing them than I was spending with my son and at work. Although I never thought I'd be a stay-at-home mom, my struggles to find childcare made me realize I was probably the best one to take care of him. Just making the decision to do so was a huge relief.

One reason I think it's important to think about childcare before you decide whether you want to have a child is to understand the realities about the challenges in finding someone. And, if you do decide to have a child, try to find one while you are pregnant. Talk to family and friends. Go to nanny services. Get referrals, Interview. Check references.

Another reason why I think it's important to think of childcare before making your decision to have a child, is to consider how your pre-formed impressions of childcare may be affecting your decision. A few women I interviewed said that they were considering not having children because they had bad childcare experiences when they were growing up. One woman shared with me that she hated her babysitter and didn't like going there, but as a child she had no choice. Her sitter wasn't kind, and was verbally abusive, but as a child she didn't know how to communicate this to her mother. Now, she says she could not imagine leaving her child with a babysitter because of her bad experience, and would have to stay home. But, because she has to work, she doesn't see how she could have a child.

If you plan ahead and are able to find a safe and loving option, it makes your decision a bit easier. One woman who was a few months pregnant told me she started calling around immediately, and through girlfriend references, found a very good professional nanny. Many times a nanny will work with a family until the children start school. So, if you can find one who is ready to leave a family, and she is looking for a long-term arrangement, it can work out well. Another woman told me how she became a member of a women's e-mail network in Los Angeles. When she found out she was pregnant, she sent out a request for a nanny. Because Los Angeles is a large city, there are many more professional childcare provider options. She had time to find someone she felt comfortable with, who had great references from her current family. A little planning can make a huge difference.

The cost of childcare depends on how many hours you need someone. And, it can be pricey – up to $10,000 to $12,000 for full-time day care at a center, to about $14,000 for a live-in au pair, to $36,000 or more for a full-time professional nanny. Some wealthier people will even pay upwards of $90,000. That is why some women decide to stay home. When they weigh the cost of childcare, how much money they make at their job, and the fact that they will be spending time away from their child, some opt to stay home. The trade off – paying money to have someone watch your child while you work (especially if it's a job that you don't particularly care for) – isn't one that makes sense to some working moms.

When you work and you need childcare

As I mentioned in the previous chapter about careers, research has shown that children suffer no emotional, behavioral, or developmental issues if a woman works, as long as the mother is warm and responsive to her child. It enhances the situation if the child is in quality childcare. Quality care differs depending on a child's stage of development. Babies need love and affection—lots of holding and interaction. Toddlers need room to safely roam and explore. Or depending on your child's temperament, they may like different educational approaches, like Montessori or Waldorf. These days, there are so many choices. It just takes time to understand your child's needs and finding the best environment where they can thrive.

QUESTION:

If you knew that you had an exceptional childcare provider that would help you after you had a child and would be there to give you a break when you needed it, would you be more likely to have a child?

---

9. RELATIONSHIPS:

How Do Your Relationships With Your Partner, Family, Friends, Employer and Co-workers Affect Your Decision to Have a Child?

The four main relationships that more than likely will be affected when a person has a child are those with their partner, extended family, friends, and co-workers. Having a child is a major life change, and these relationships will undergo transitions. Understanding these possible changes beforehand allows you to make an informed decision about whether you want a child, and if you do, to prepare for these changes in advance, making the transition a bit smoother.

How having a child may affect your relationship

How a child affects a couple's relationship is a major concern for many people when deciding whether to have a child, and for a good reason.

Here's the bad news. There have been several studies that show marital satisfaction in a relationship decreases after the birth of a child. One study shows that satisfaction declines by 20 to 50%, and another shows a 70% drop.[1] Research shows that 70% of couples say they feel "very unhappy" after a baby is born.[2]

But why? What causes parents to feel this way? In one study which followed about 200 couples for eight years after their marriage, 90% of couples said their relationship was worse after their first baby. The researchers learned that following the birth of the first child, communication between

parents became a huge problem, including increased criticism, withdrawal, and self-reported lack of communication. Couples also felt a decrease in confidence that the marriage would last.[3]

Other couples reported eight times more conflict in their marriages after the baby joins the family. Problems that are commonly mentioned are distance in the relationship, spouse doesn't help with the kids, not having enough sex, not paying attention to spouse, aloneness in relationship, and no time for relationship because busy with kids, work, and personal interests.[4] If there's not enough time for parent to replenish their relationship, they get disconnected.

It's not really the child that is causing these difficulties, but rather how the parents handle their transition to becoming a parent. Having a child is a major change in lifestyle. People are tested and challenged in ways they may have never expected, especially if they haven't spent much time with children. And, it's not a situation that people can really prepare for because you don't know what kind of baby you are going to get. It's not easy to gage how having a child will impact your life or how you'll react and adjust. When a child joins a family, parents spend the first few months, and even years, getting used to a new way of life. There's sleep deprivation and fatigue. And, it can be stressful learning new things—like how to care of a baby—no matter how much a baby is wanted and loved.

Being aware beforehand that relationship problems can arise gives couples the opportunity to mentally prepare and be conscientious of their behavior so that they can recognize issues before they become unmanageable. Among suggestions that may help ease the transition to parenthood is to remember to communicate positively with each other. Be honest with how much you can handle and work to solve the issues together. Find time together and for yourself. Alone-time and solitude give parents time to recharge. And, having

some help and support truly makes a difference. When parents know that they have someone to help watch and care for their child, it can give them the peace of mind to feel free to care for themselves, recharge, and also spend time together as a couple.

One father, who was interviewed in an article about the strain a child can put on a relationship, shared that he didn't handle the first few years of his daughter's birth well. He said he couldn't adjust to the needs and demands placed on him and his wife. He missed his wife's attention because she was focused on caring for their daughter. He said he had an affair. But once his daughter got a few years older and he could communicate and interact with her, he started to appreciate and enjoy family life. But it was too late, and his marriage ended. His advice for new parents is, "For the first five years, don't cheat on each other. Do not lie to each other. Just stick it out."

A mother of two boys, who had plenty of experience being a mother, told me that her third baby boy had colic and wouldn't stop crying. She and her husband checked into every medical option for the crying, and were told, "It's colic." She said every evening she feared bedtime. She and her husband took turns holding their son. This evening ritual, of course, took a toll on their relationship. As the nights wore on, the more tired they got and the less civil they became toward one another, causing more arguments and hurt feelings. She didn't know what else to do and called her mother who lived in a different state for advice. Her mother reassured them to just hold the baby, give him love, and reminded them that the baby's colic is a just a phase he's going through and it will pass. Hearing that the colic was a phase and would pass, for some reason, made their evening rituals seem much more tolerable. Although this may sound extreme to some, the couple called her mother every night for about a month so that she could

remind them "it is a stage and will pass." They didn't feel so alone, and felt that they had support. Eventually, the colic did pass.

Babies go through many different phases in their first three years of life – from sleeping through the night, to getting first teeth, to crawling, walking, talking, and learning how to use the bathroom all by themselves. Remembering that some of the more challenging phases won't last can help a new parent cope with their new role.

Here's the good news. According to that study that followed 200 couples for 8 years of marriage, having a baby does bring on sudden and dramatic change in a relationship, but after eight years of marriage, there isn't much difference between parents and those couples without children. After eight years of togetherness, relationships with kids or without tend to have the same level of satisfaction.[5]

Not all couple's relationships suffer. Other studies have shown that 15% of fathers and 7% of mothers ended up more satisfied with their marriage after birth.[6] Couples who have an easier time adjusting to children list good communication as one of the main characteristics that help them during their transition. Another study shows that about one-third to one-half of couples experienced more stability, increases in relationship satisfaction, or more love from the transition to parenthood.[7]

Another indication of how a couple adjusts to parenthood depends on how long they've been married prior to having children, the parents' family of origin, and how religious they are. Research has shown that if a couple was married longer before having a child, their relationship fared better than others. It is assumed that the couple had time to work out household responsibilities and structure financial priorities before a child is born.

Poor functioning in an individual's family of origin has been shown to predict declines in both marital satisfaction and communication after a child is born. And, the more religious someone is, the less impact the transition to parenthood has on marital satisfaction. Highly religious mothers experience a greater sense of satisfaction after birth than those who are less religious.

It is evident that as a society we don't do enough "relationship" preparation before a baby comes into our lives. To make it easier, remember that relationships require effort. Ignoring or avoiding the fact that your relationship will change after you have a child won't help. You will probably have to learn how to do things differently. One of the main skills to work on is communication. Don't act like everything is fine when things aren't. If you feel disconnected from your partner, start by physically connecting—hold hands and hug. Show each other appreciation so you both feel valued and appreciated. Give each other three compliments a day to help you focus on the positive. Look for the good, overlook more of the bad. Hiring good childcare and support will give you the chance so you can have time together. There are ways to make any situation better.

And what about sex, sex, sex?

A concern of couples when thinking about how a child will impact their relationship is how their sex life will be affected. Couples worry that they will have less sex, no sex, not enjoy sex anymore, or lose that intimate connection with that person they love. Why is sex so important? Because when couples were asked to rank which attribute was important for a successful marriage, "Happy sexual relationship," was ranked the second highest attribute with a 70% rating, right after

"Faithfulness," with a 93% rating.[8] Sex ranked higher than "Children," which ranked second to last, with a 41% rating.

So how does having children affect a couple's sex life? Studies have shown that there is little agreement on when sexual activity resumes after childbirth. One report found that at about five to seven weeks postpartum, about 50% of women had started having sex again.[9] Another study showed that most women (up to 86% according to some studies) experience some level of sexual problems postpartum.[10]

Numerous reasons for the delay in resumption of sex after childbirth have been suggested. The principal ones are: taking enough time to heal after giving birth; childcare is time consuming and tiring, leaving little energy for sex; pain related to an episiotomy; and discomfort related to inadequate lubrication of the vagina due to low levels of estrogen postpartum.[11]

Because birth experiences vary and everyone is different, the amount of time it takes for a woman to be physically and emotionally ready for, and even interested in, sex postpartum can range from several weeks to several months. For women who've had c-sections, it's recommended that they wait for at least 4 to 6 weeks. Some may wait longer, from 8 to 12 weeks, if they've had a high-risk pregnancy or have had an emergency cesarean after a long, trying labor. Women who suffer extensive perineal tearing that required a large episiotomy may not be "comfortable" for several months after the birth. Of course, women have to listen to their bodies and do what is right for them and take as long as they need.

These postpartum sexual issues are some of the reasons some women have shared with me that they would prefer to have an elective c-section. Women worried about the stretching of their vagina or episiotomies, which may diminish their sexual self-confidence and enjoyment, would rather have an elective c-section than risk the chance of vaginal tearing during birth. One report shows that episiotomies occur in about 35% of vaginal births in the United States.[12] Others studies say the rate of episiotomies is more like 40%, with some hospitals reporting a rate of 73%.[13][14] And, 31% of female OB-GYNs interviewed for a medical journal in Britain said they'd select an elective c-section for themselves even if they had no medical reason for one.[15]

Being concerned how your sexual relationship with your partner will be affected is not something to ignore. For many couples, it's one of the foundations for a happy and successful marriage. Having an awareness of how women are affected by giving birth can help couples prepare and handle the changes they may encounter.

Misperceptions about "normal" sex life

When people think of how their sex life will be affected postpartum, I think that most people have a misperception of what having a "normal" sex life entails, especially when it comes to the amount of sex people think they should be having. We are inundated by the media's constant portrayal that everyone is having sex all the time, and advertisements for Viagra® remind us that anyone can have sex by just popping a pill. These ever-present reminders can cause one to think that if we aren't having sex at least once a day, something must be wrong with us and skew our expectations higher than what happens in reality.

Let me put sex in perspective for you. I learned that just prior to marriage (or that start of a serious relationship) and during the first few years of marriage is when couples have the most amount of sex.[16] It is also during that time—usually the first five years of marriage—that couples have their first child. It makes sense. The more sex you have, the more likely that you'll get pregnant. In a way, it's the nature of the early stages of a relationship—the honeymoon affect—that causes people to believe that having that much sex is the norm, and it is, for that stage of a relationship. However, there is a tendency that the longer the relationship progresses and as both parties in the relationship age, the amount of sex naturally decreases.

For example, research shows that married couples between the ages of 18 to 29 have sex about 109 times a year, or two times a week. Those not married in the same age group had sex 73.4 times a year. Among the married, the amount of sex drops from 109 times per year for those under 30 to 87 times per year for those between 30 to 39, to 70 times for those between 40 to 49, and then about 17 times per year for those 70 and older. This pattern prevails both for husbands and wives, with women usually having less sex then men overall. As unmarried people age, the amount of sex drops, as well. The normal trend is for people to have sex as they get older.

Average amount of sex per year, by age		
Age	Married	Unmarried
18-29	109.1	73.4
30-39	87	67.8
40-49	70.2	48.2
50-59	52.5	29.3
60-69	32.2	16.2
70+	17.2	3.3

SOURCE: American Sexual Behavior: Trends, Socio-Demographic Differences and Risk Behavior, March 2006.

Nonetheless, people are all different, and if they want more sex, they can do something about it. One gentleman I spoke to told me that he was married to his first wife for 15 years and had two children with her. But during this time, they grew apart and divorced. He said one reason he wasn't happy in the relationship was that they didn't have much sex. Then he met a woman 10 years younger than himself, and he wanted to make sure that she was open to having more sex. They ended up marrying and having one child. And, because they both made sex a priority in their marriage, they are enjoying an active sex life.

The decline of sex in marriages is rather normal and can be explained by several factors. The waning of the honeymoon effect in relationships is one factor. But the main cause is age. Age reduces hormonal output, can bring about or exacerbate health issues, and increase the chances of impotence, all of which can impede the amount of sex one has. Even those who rate their marriages as very happy and who still say they are in love have less sex as they age. And, because of familiarity, the quality of sexual activity declines with long-term relationships, which contributes to the reduced amount. However, all studies show that married people have more sex than unmarried, single, and currently divorced people.

Another survey of 16,000 adult Americans in confidential face-to-face interviews shows that people aren't having sex as much as the media portrays. According to these interviews, the average American has sex approximately 2 to 3 times a month. Even among those under 40 years old, the median individual has sex once a week. For those Americans under 40, only 10% say they have sex at least four times a week, and up to 10% say they are celibate. Of those Americans 40 years and older, 25% say they are celibate. And 32% of American women over 40 report they did not have sex in the previous year.[17]

So, keep the results of these studies and facts in mind when making your decision. Whether or not you have a child, there is a good chance that the amount of sex you have in your relationship will naturally decrease as time goes on and you age. Of course, we are all free to create the lifestyles we want. And, if you do desire more sex in your life—with our without children—it's something that you probably have to make a priority. Giving birth may not be easy for all women. Understanding what they've endured and how it can affect them, hopefully, will help their partners be kinder and more patient postpartum.

Your relationships with extended family

Another concern people have is how having a child will affect their relationship with their extended family. Some families are more family-oriented than others and make the effort to build a solid foundation with its members. They are welcoming and supportive of the new parents, and the family actively helps and participates in the lives of the child. I've also been told stories of how having children has brought families together—that parents who were once distant and aloof may see life differently once they become grandparents and transform into people who are more willing to work on their relationship with their own children for the sake of the grandchildren.

However, not all are like that. I've also been told many stories from parents about how their children's grandparents are uninterested and uninvolved in their children's lives. Some ascribe to the, "I raised mine, you raise yours," philosophy of grandparenting. They send the obligatory gift at birthday and holidays, but really make no effort to have a relationship with that child or children. Even those who came from traditional and close families found that once they had their own children, they were on their own.

Nicole shared her experience about her mother who doesn't help her at all. She said it wouldn't be so bad, except that Nicole remembers when she was growing up that her grandmother (her mother's mother) was always there to help her mother. She wonders if her mother even remembers how much help she had. Nicole said that her grandmother would come over to babysit, or take them to her house, or sometimes take them out to the movies or just to run errands. She said they had a relationship with her and loved her dearly. However, her own mother does none of this with her children. And when she asks for help, her mother responds like it's such a burden she just doesn't ask anymore.

Another mother shared with me that when her young son became extremely sick with a life threatening illness and had to be in and out of the hospital for a few years, her mother never once came to the hospital to help her.

Several other mothers expressed the same pattern of grandmothers who helped their mothers, but now their mothers aren't willing to do the same for their daughters.

Then again, there are extended families who can be very helpful and supportive. Several people I interviewed told me that they moved back "home" to be closer to their parents. Sometimes, the parents moved to be closer to their grandchildren. They didn't realize how important family was to them until they had their children and made efforts to bring the extended family together.

Jennifer grew up in Iowa and moved to Washington, DC, after college, where she obtained a job in a research think tank. She ended up meeting her husband in DC, and it turned out he was also from Iowa. They had two children, 2 and 4 years old, when they decided to return to Iowa to be near family. Jennifer told me it just got too difficult to do everything with no support. So they moved back to Iowa, and both sets of grandparents and their siblings all help and are involved with their son and daughter. She said being near family has made their life easier. They are less stressed and happier.

Other parents shared how grandparents helped them out by picking up children from school, taking them to activities, and watching them on the weekend so the parents could have a little downtime to themselves or actually spend time together. One grandma I met told me that she picks up her granddaughter from school twice a week and takes her ice skating and then they spend the evening together until her parents pick her up after work. She said it gives her great pleasure to spend time with her granddaughter. Another grandma told me that "Thursdays" are her time with her grandson, and she also picks him up from school so that she can spend the afternoon with him.

A study in Britain showed that grandparents who are involved in the upbringing of their grandchildren can contribute to a child's well-being. The factors that predicted grandparent involvement included living in a less deprived area, frequent contact, and good health of the grandparent. The children surveyed didn't find proximity as being important since they use modern technology to communicate—like Skype. The children said they felt closer to their grandparents when they undertook some traditional parenting tasks.[18] Another study conducted in Europe found that maternal grandparents are more willing to travel further in order to sustain frequent (daily or a few times a week) contact with their grandchildren than paternal grandparents. The researchers conclude that family related through their mothers matter more than those through their fathers. [19]

So when thinking of your family when deciding whether to have children or not, take some time to understand your expectations of them and if they are even realistic. If you think that you will have family support, it can be very helpful and make your life a lot easier. On the other hand, if you don't have family help, understand that you'll probably be doing everything yourself and have to find support from others. But, you don't need to have a close external family to still enjoy your child and create your own family unit. As one famous life coach told me after I had my child, they (the extended family members you may not get along with or see at all) don't matter as much after you have your child—especially when you just focus on the love you have for your child and do best by him or her.

Your relationship with friends

The friendships you have prior to having children will more than likely change after you have a child, especially with friends who don't have children. In a study of 4,000 mothers of young children, about 50% said they lost contact with one set of friends, but gained even more after having their child.[20] Prior to having children, these moms said they had about 3 close friends—one who was close and two out of "habit." But, after having a child, new mothers increase their friend count by eight.

One reason why friendships fade, especially with those who don't have kids, is that they can't relate to the lifestyle change and the demands placed on new parents. A new mother is so preoccupied taking care of an infant that she doesn't have time for her friends. She barely has time for herself. But, the changing of friends isn't unusual. As we go through life and have different experiences, our friendships evolved and change. Having a child is just another one of those times. The survey showed that 6 out of 10 moms felt that other mothers were more in tune with their thinking and behavior than their friends who don't have children.[21]

New moms end up making new friends, since many will make an effort to create a group of trusted friends that they can rely on in a time of need. In the study of 4,000 moms I mentioned previously, 48% said they focused on establishing such a group. The places where they most likely met new acquaintances were in the school playground (44%), childcare (32%), and morning coffee get-togethers (22%).[22]

When I discovered that I was pregnant, I did develop new friendships with women who helped me through. Many of my childfree friends, understandably, couldn't give me advice about tests, doctors, and hospitals. These moms came to my rescue and gave me advice and made referrals. It was a huge help. I still have many childfree friends, and I do like to hear about their work and travels, but my circle has also expanded to include mothers who can relate to my experiences, as well. And I do meet more people because of my son's activities. Some of these people are acquaintances and some have become friends. Since my son has started school, we are meeting and engaging with more people than we would have otherwise.

When thinking about your decision to have children, remember that your friendships will probably change if you do have children. But the good friendships will always be there, no matter what. You will only make more friends, thanks to your child's influence.

Your relationship with co-workers

When at work, we have certain duties and responsibilities that we must maintain to work well with our co-workers and, of course, to remain employed. When deciding to have a child, some people consider how their work situation and co-workers may be affected. Several factors can influence how your work life will be impacted: the type of profession or job you have, your level of responsibility, whether you are part of team, the corporate environment and culture you work in, the maternity leave and lifestyle policies where you work, and the personalities or your co-workers.

One of the biggest complaints that co-workers have with people who have children is that they feel like they have to pick up the slack when a parent has to stay home because a child is sick and when a parent leaves early for a school function or take a child to a doctor's appointment. Childfree co-workers feel that they have to cover for a parent while they are occupied, attending to their childcare responsibilities. Some have even claimed that parents don't work as long or as hard, take advantage of others, shirk their duties, and shouldn't have children if they can't live up to their responsibilities.

During my interviews, I'd hear co-workers complain about their parent counterparts, and then the conversation would turn to an "us vs. them" or "childfree vs. parent" type of discussion. It doesn't have to be this way. Companies do provide paid time off that both childfree and parents. Both groups should feel free to use the time as they wish. I have spoken to parents who don't take their time away from work lightly. Most parents are conscientious of their performance at work. After all, they have a family to support and losing a job could be catastrophic.

QUESTIONS:

A. **Partner:** What's the longest you've ever went without sex as an adult? Could you go without sex for six months if you had to?

B. **Family:** What are your expectations with family involvement and help? How involved would you want them to be? What is realistic? If your mother said that she'd help you watch your child, would that be a "good" thing?

C. **Friends:** Do you have a friend who's had a child? How did your relationship change? Usually, common experiences join people together. Reflect upon your life and the friends you've had and currently have. Where and how did you meet them? What if all your friends disappeared tomorrow? Poof! How would you cope?

D. **Co-workers:** What would you do in these situations, when you have a meeting to attend in 30 minutes?

- The school calls to tell you that your child has a scraped his leg, or has a fever, or is vomiting?

- Your pet that you've had for 6 years cut itself or is sick and throwing up?

- Your boyfriend or girlfriend was just in a car accident, and although doesn't need to go to the hospital, is quite shaken up?

10. BENEFITS:

What are the Good Things About Having Children?

Earlier in this book, I explained how human brains tend to focus on the negative in order to protect us from harms that can cause us difficulties or put us in danger. We do this for survival purposes. When it comes to making a decision about having a child, we may get stuck focusing on those aspects of having children that will make our life different or difficult and not be able to see the "positives" or benefits. That is why I included a separate section for the good reasons to have children. There are people that I interviewed who had such a positive view and truly loved children that it was a pleasure talking to them, even though a part of me wondered if they were really being honest. But studies show, that when parents are asked why they decided to have their first (or only) child, 87% said, "The joy of having children." [1]

One thing to keep in mind when considering the benefits of having children is to understand how the mixed messages we receive about motherhood can tarnish the experience we have of being with and enjoying children. Motherhood has gone from a "glorified" position as one of the most important roles a woman could undertake to just one of many options—an option that doesn't look very appealing. Many women in the past felt that they were misled by the idealization of motherhood, or daughters witnessed their mothers struggle and decided that motherhood isn't all that grand.

Over the past decade, books started to appear to discuss the realities of motherhood to ensure that women aren't misled again, or feel shocked or impaired if they struggled with their new role. In 2000, Susan Maushart, an Australian columnist and mother of three, wrote *The Mask of Motherhood: How Being a Mother Changes Our Lives and Why We Never Talk About It*, where she explained that mothers need to start talking about how difficult motherhood is, not only to maintain their own sanity, but so that women can identify the issues that are creating difficulty in order to make improvements.

Other books followed. In 2001, Ann Crittendden's *The Price of Motherhood: Why the Most Important Job in the World is Still the Least Valued* explained how the workplace and family life are at odds and how the United States and its companies lag behind many other developed countries in providing support to its mothers and families. Then in 2004, *The Mommy Myth: The Idealization of Motherhood and How It Has Undermined All Women*, by Susan Douglas and Meredith Michaels, shared how the media pushes an idealized version of the perfect mother, causing women to try to meet an unreachable standard and pitting stay-at-home moms versus working moms as to who is doing best for their children. Then in 2006, Judith Warner's *Perfect Madness; Mothering in the Age of Anxiety* explained how middle-class families struggle with parenting and family life due to economic and social policies that aren't supportive.

All of these books, and there are more, show that the society we live in, and the economic and social policies that people attempt to and are forced to parent in makes having a child and being a mother so difficult in these modern times.. The reason I bring this up in the "benefits of having a child" section is to help people realize that the enjoyment you get from your child or family can be tarnished or corrupted by the need to respond to the society we live in. Today, more people are unemployed, are struggling financially, and live with uncertain futures. More women work to support their families, and the ability to stay at home with their children is not really an option anymore, except for the very wealthy. More people are focusing on how to make money to support themselves and don't have the time or energy to devote to having or raising a family. If you can't provide for yourself, how can you take care of a family? All these external stresses do diminish our experiences with our children and can make having children feel more difficult than it is.

Also, when I interviewed people who didn't have children, some people said they didn't see many positives to having a child and that was one of their main reservations in having them. Before I had a child, I felt the same way. I remember going to a work-related leadership seminar. When we introduced ourselves, we were told to share our greatest achievement with the group. About 75% of the participants said that having their child or children was their greatest achievement. I was dumbfounded and thought these people lived sheltered lives.

I really didn't see or read a lot about the positives of having children before I had my son. Two friends who had children in their mid-twenties—one while in law school and the other a few years out of graduate school—told me not to have children. They said it was too hard and advised me to enjoy my freedom.

Yet, another friend who had a child a few years after graduate school could not understand my ambivalence. She couldn't wait to have children and told me after she had two children that, "Your life has more purpose and a deeper meaning after having children." At the time, I could not relate to what she shared. As with most things in life, it's difficult to know how something feels until you actually do it. Now, I get it.

Comments from people who were skeptical about having children

Below are some stories from women and men who try to put their profound feelings into words and to help share with you the joys and benefits that they experienced by becoming parents. They write about love, purpose, change, connection to the world and transformation.

Dr. Sharon L.
**Doctorate from Columbia University,
Leadership Expert and Executive Coach,
and mother of Joshua (6):**

Love. Did I truly know it before having a child? No. I thought love was getting what I wanted and doing what I wanted each day. I thought it was about only getting my needs met. The operative words here are "I", "me," "Mine." Love was about "me," "myself," and "I." When I had my son, I started to reframe my definition of love. I started to learn about service. I started to learn what "give and you shall receive" truly meant. Perhaps the reason for existence was not all about "me," "myself" and "I." There is only so far I can go in creating a life that is all based on me getting what I want and doing what I want each day.

Many people, once they reach retirement and do what they want each day, get bored after six months to a year.

I never knew the type of love I experience when I look at my son, and my heart hurts with how much I love him. I never knew the kind of love I now know that would make me run in front of a speeding truck to save my son. I would gladly give my life for his if I needed to.

I never knew the inner strength I had to form and continue to form on a day to day basis when I am tired at the end of a long work day and my son needs me. I have had to learn how to respond with love and not anger. I have had to learn to tap inside to energy reserves I never knew I had.

I won't lie. Life was much easier before I had my son. I did whatever I wanted, whenever I wanted to, yet there was always a sense of emptiness inside me. I wouldn't trade that ease for this love any day. I believe a key purpose for us as human beings on this planet is to learn to love. For me, I never would have learned this without my son.

When asked to write something positive about having a child, the first word that came into my heart and mind was LOVE. Thank you my sweet Joshua for helping me learn more about love. And for helping me receive so many blessings from giving to you. Through loving you, I have become so much more of who I truly am.

Robin W.
MBA in International Business, Executive Recruiter in Healthcare, and mother of Maddie (12) and Phillip (11):

My children have defined my life in a way that I can't adequately describe but that strikes to the core of what I believe is a higher purpose. The often used analogy of "It's like your heart walking around outside of your body," is so very true....whether experiencing their trials with them, watching them develop and learn new things, or even dropping them off at sleep away camp for the first time. All these experiences that fill you with such a profound combination of pride, joy, excitement for them, and yes, also loss as they continue to gain independence.

Motherhood takes you outside of yourself and creates a more empathetic, giving, and naturally protective bent to all you do, and ultimately, confirms "it's not all about me" and reaffirms

215

the very significant responsibility of raising good children and citizens. This means kind, caring, empathetic, goal-oriented, self-reliant, and honest children who will in turn do the same for theirs. It is the most difficult journey—one filled with endless missteps and also rewards—large and small. Although I always knew motherhood was a key component of what I wanted in life, I never could have guessed how quickly I came to barely recall my life prior Madeleine and Phillip.

Lastly, I wake up every day not only with gratitude for their health and well-being, but gratitude to them as individuals for making me a better person and loving me so unconditionally. It is a privilege to share their lives and usher them through this journey we all share.

Jamie M.
Writer, and mother of a boy (1):

When people used to try to tell us how radically our lives would change if we had a child, we both felt a sense of panic. We liked our lives! We didn't want them to change that much— couldn't we have a baby and live pretty much the same way? Well, our son just turned one, and so far, anyway, the answer is: no. But what no one really explained to us was that we would actually WANT to change because of the insane love we felt for our child.

When you look objectively at what will be different - you will have less money, less free time, less time for travel and creative pursuits and WAY less sleep - it sounds like a bum deal. But it is impossible to understand ahead of time how deeply in love you will fall with your child once he is a real person and not a theoretical concept, and how that love makes the equation make sense. We actually prefer to hang out with our son than to do almost anything else - we call him our "new favorite person" - so the missed movies, concerts and dinners with friends from the last year feel like small potatoes. We do take him out with us a lot, with whatever friends will tolerate a 6pm dinner. It isn't always easy to have a 'normal' adult conversation at those dinners, and I hope that this will get easier and easier after a while—but for now, the trade-off is, in retrospect, a no-brainer. Bring on the change—he's adorable!

Liesl J.
Writer and author of www.mamalog.com, and mother of Lucas (4):

I can no longer imagine a life where I'm not a mother to my 4-year-old son, Lucas. But there was a time, a long time, when I couldn't imagine making room for children. I put off motherhood for many years focusing instead on my career and marriage. My husband and I waited 12 years to be "ready" to have our first child. But even so, I was blindsided by the shock of becoming a mother. And yet today, I can appreciate this opportunity I've been given to rise to the challenge of parenting.

From the moment my body started taking over during pregnancy, I was stripped of whatever illusions I held of being in control of my life. Having a child has pulled me time and time again out of my comfort zones, forcing me to act without a plan. I remember first weeks with a newborn trying to chart his routine, to schedule feedings and sleep, and eventually laughing at the ridiculousness of it all and allowing his rhythm to emerge. In doing so, I began to listen to my gut, to trust my instincts, to allow life to unfold and trust that I would have what I needed to cope. And I did.

Parenting has taught me what I can bear and I found out that it's much more than I actually expected of myself. I've worked a lot harder and slept a lot less, but accomplished more than ever since becoming a mom because I've learned to make every minute count. It's demanded that I step up, that I take on the ultimate responsibility of protecting life, knowing that I face the potential of failure on a daily basis. It's humbled my burgeoning ego and forced me to shift my perspectives to allow for a world much bigger and more important than my own.

And it's connected me to that bigger world, too. If I die today, I have left my legacy through my son. When I look into his face, I see myself reflected, for better or worse. I realize that he will carry my genes, my lips, and whatever I have taught him (good or bad), with him throughout his life. Becoming a parent has connected me to other parents, facing their own mountains and demons as they raise their children. It's connected me to my own parents, my husband's parents, my brother—seeing them now as parents, too. I appreciate the quote by Elizabeth Stone: "Making the decision to have a child—it's momentous. It is to decide forever to have your heart go walking around outside your body." Now I see them everywhere, these parents like me, their hearts outside them.

Once you're a parent, the way you live your life can never ever be the same. It's being distracted all the time by that pull of your child, conscious or not. It's life where laziness and carelessness are no longer options. You feel held to a higher standard every moment, by society, family, other parents, and mostly, by yourself. In a life where every action and word is mimicked and adopted by your child, you are inspired to be a role model every second. Ambitions for career, money, or whatever was important before are replaced by the desire to be a better mother, a better person.

I am a better person because I've been given the gift of Lucas, the privilege of calling myself his mother. I never knew love like this existed, this love that is an invisible cord between us, powerful and ever present. He honors me with his love—so pure, his devotion—so centered on me, and his trust—so complete. And I am humbled to be his parent, wondering sometimes who is really guiding whom.

Other benefits people mentioned

Other parents that I interviewed said having a child allowed them to see the world through new eyes. As adults, we take the simplest things for granted, whereas for a toddler, that rock or flower is a new experience. They are curious about all those items that have grown mundane to us. Seeing their wonderment in the simplest things can make us stop and appreciate the world anew.

One father shared that his values and priorities changed. He said control over his own time became more of a priority after he had a child and that he was inspired to start his own business by opening a franchise. Another father left his consulting job and wanted to work in alternative energy. He said he cared more about the future of the planet since his son was born and wants to make it a better world for him to live in.

Another mother shared that she was inspired to lose 120 pounds after she had her daughter. She said that she didn't want her daughter to grow up with a bad role model and chose to eat healthy and exercise to set an example. Some other moms became inspired to improve the food offered through their child's school lunch program.

Other people have told me about how they became more considerate and thoughtful to others. As one mother explained, "Everyone is someone's child, which means that since I'm a mom now, and know what it feels like to love a child, I want my child to be treated kindly by others. I'm sure other mothers feel the same way – wanting their child to be treated well. Now when I interact with people, I make more of an effort to treat them as I'd want my son treated. I think my son has made me a kinder person."

A father told me having children gives him a reason to go biking, boating, and hiking more. He's always like these activities, but now he feels that he has more justification to do so. Alternatively, a mother told me that she will use her children as an excuse to get out of doing things she's not interested in doing. If she's invited to a function that doesn't seem interesting, but doesn't want to offend her inviter, she will use her child as an excuse.

Before having children, a girlfriend and I were at a resort, sipping wine, discussing life, and we said that if we died right then, we'd be fine with it. We'd have no regrets. We felt we had achieved a certain level of accomplishments and felt quite fulfilled. We got to live life, pursue our education, fall in love, and travel. But after we had children, our perspectives changed. Of course, we haven't been to that resort and sipped wine together for what seems like forever. We've been busy with kids and work. And, now, we don't even want to think of going anywhere, especially dying! We want to be around to take care of our sons and see how they grow and develop and experience life with them. We have important work to do. We also know that our children need us, at least for now.

It may be difficult to relate to the benefits of having a child, especially when they are unknowable, immeasurable, intangible, and emotional. There is nothing else to compare the experience to unless you do it. As with anything in life, anything you do requires work and effort, and there are pros and cons to everything. Parenting is hard work, but there are many people out there who can tell you about the benefits. And, because there are so many, you've got to believe that they all can't be lying.

QUESTION:

What are three benefits or "good reasons" to have a child? If you can't think of any, it may be an indication that you are only focusing on the negative. As with most things in life, there are positive and negative sides to every circumstance—even having a child. And, if you are being objective, you probably can figure out aspects for both sides of the situation.

11. AM I THE CHILDFREE TYPE?

He used to say to me: 'Anybody can be a father or a husband.
There are only five people in the world who can do what I do,
and I'm going for that.'
Linda Hamilton in an interview with the *Daily Mail Online*
about her ex-husband James Cameron, producer of Avatar and
the Terminator movies

Not having children is on the rise

For those of you considering not having children, you will not be alone. As I've mentioned in various parts of this book, more people are determining NOT to have children and fertility rates are falling in almost all developed countries. There are still many people having children, but if you choose not to have any, you are no longer an anomaly. It is more common and understandable for people not to have children. All the people I interviewed did not think that you need to have a child to have a fulfilling life.

And, more professional, successful women and men are acknowledging that they aren't interested in having children – Oprah Winfrey, Helen Mirren, Cameron Diaz, Rachel Ray, Danica Patrick, and George Clooney are only a few. With more prominent role models voicing their preference for a childfree lifestyle, hopefully men and women who decide not to have children will realize that this option is not unusual anymore.

Cameron Diaz, Actress:

"I think women are afraid to say that they don't want children because they're going to get shunned. But I think that's changing now. I have more girlfriends who don't have kids than those that do. And honestly? We don't need any more kids. We

have plenty of people on this planet." In *Cosmopolitan Magazine,* June, 11, 2009

"Having children changes your life drastically, and I really love my life," she says. "Children aren't the only things that bring you gratification and happiness, and it's easier to give life than to give love, so I don't know. That kind of change would have to be either very well thought out, or a total mistake – a real oops!" July 2010 issue of *InStyle Magazine.*

Danica Patrick (29), Professional Race Car Driver:

"I think it is something which is probably not for me at this point and realistically, I don't know what point that would ever be. My focus is on racing and of course I have a lot of outside interests which take up my time."

"I am not someone who has a strong yearning for kids at all," she told *USA Today. "I see all my friends with kids. I will get up at 10 AM and text them and they'll say 'Ha, funny. One of my sons was in my room at 5:30 in the morning so I can't say I slept until 10.' That's just their life." I think more all the time that it looks hard, that looks like something I am not ready for and doesn't interest me at this point."* Interview with *Yahoo! Sports,* March 2011.

Oprah Winfrey in a 2004 interview with Barbara Walters on ABC:

Barbara: I interviewed you in 1988. And you said, and I quote, "I want to be there loving and nurturing my daughter or son.

Oprah: Uh-huh!

Barbara: You've given up the idea of having a daughter or a son. Why?

Oprah: I've given it up because I feel like that's not a part of what I was born to do. It just wasn't right for me. And I'm so okay with it. And I do feel that, in many ways that the world's children, the community's children, are my children. I feel like I can be a voice for children who don't or are not allowed to speak for themselves."

More and more people are interested in the childfree lifestyle. Over the past ten years, more and more books have been written by people who have decided not to have children. Their reasoning and rational can be found in them. In fact, there are more books written about NOT having children than helping people figure out if they want to have a child.

- *Complete Without Kids: An Insider's Guide to Childfree Living By Choice or By Chance*, by Ellen L. Walker, Jan. 11, 2011.
- *Kids or No Kids*, by Zoe Slater, April 11. 2011.
- *I'm Taking My Eggs and Going Home: How One Woman Dared to Say No To Motherhood*, by Lisa Manterfield, Nov. 20, 2010.
- *No Way Baby! Explaining, Understanding & Defending the Decision Not to Have Children*, by Karen Foster, Nov. 15, 2010.
- *Two is Enough: A Couple's Guide to Living Childless by Choice*, by Laura S. Scott, Oct. 27, 2009.
- *No Kids: 40 Good Reasons Not To Have Children*, by Corine Maier, Aug. 4, 2009.
- *Childfree Women: Becoming, Being & Belonging*, by Lisa Mortimor, Jan. 20, 2009.
- *Childfree & Loving It!* by Nicki Defago, June 29, 2007.
- *Pride & Joy: The Lives & Passions of Women Without Children,* by Terri Casey, Apr. 13. 2007.
- *Baby Not On Board: A Celebration of Life Without Kids,* by Jennifer L. Shawn, July 7, 2005.

- *The Childless Revolution: What It Means To Be Childless Today*, by Madelyn Cain, Apr. 2, 2002
- *Family of Two: Interviews With Happily Married Couples Without Children by Choice*, by Laura Carroll and Krista Bartz, Sept. 21, 2000
- *Child-Free Zone: Why More People Are Choosing Not To Be Parents*, by Susan Moore and David Moore, June 1, 2000.
- *The Chosen Lives of Childfree Men*, by Patricia W. Lunneborg, 1999
- *Beyond Motherhood: Choosing a Life Without Children*, by Jeanne Safer, Feb. 1, 1996.

In this Childfree section, I refer to Laura Scott's book, *Two is Enough*, on a few occasions. I do so because she is the founder of the Childless by Choice Project, which includes a research project, book, and documentary that explores the motives and decision-making process behind the choice to remain childless, and she has studied and surveyed the childfree extensively.[1] Compared to many of the other books written on the subject, hers includes research and data to explain the childfree viewpoint.

Who are the childfree?

The National Center of Health Statistics confirms that the percentage of women in the United States of childbearing age who define themselves as voluntary childless is on the rise: from 2.4% in 1982, to 4.3% in 1990, to 6.6% in 1995. That was about 4.1 million women saying no to motherhood in 1995.[2] More recently, the number of women between the ages of 40 and 44 who are childless has doubled from 10% in 1976 to 20% in 2006.[3] And, 46% of women in the United States aged 18 to 44 are childless as of July 2011, up from 35% in 1976. In

Canada there is a similar trend, where in a 2001 survey 7% of women and 8% of men between the ages of 20 and 34 say they intended to stay childless.

In an early book about childfree women, characteristics of women who decided not to have children were listed. These women were usually the eldest daughter in the family, who had an advanced degree. These women also said they didn't have a maternal instinct and they also valued their freedom and liked to travel. Many already helped with raising brothers and sisters and said that they already felt that they already raised children.

In Laura Scott's book, *Two is Enough*, sociologist Dr. Kristen Park explains that compared to the general population, the voluntary childless are, "more educated, more likely to have been employed in professional and managerial occupations, more likely to have both spouses earning relatively high incomes, more likely to life in urban areas, less religious, in general in less traditional role orientations and less conventional."[4]

There are also women who are childfree, even though they wanted to have children. Melanie Notkin, founder of SavvyAuntie.com and author of *Savvy Auntie: The Ultimate Guide for Cool Aunts, Great-Aunts, and Godmothers, and All Women Who Love Kids*, points out, "There is a place between motherhood and choosing not to be a mother. And tens of millions of women are there."[5] Just because a woman doesn't have kids doesn't mean she isn't maternal or doesn't like to be with kids. There are childfree women who are maternal and always thought they would have children, but because of circumstances – mainly not meeting the right person – do not. They love children and will actively make effort to have them in their lives – through being an involved aunt, a mentor, a supportive neighbor, and a pen-pal.

Why people decide not to have children

When I spoke to childfree people during my interviews the reasons they shared for not wanting children were: They didn't like or couldn't relate to children very much, had other interests they wanted to pursue, liked their freedom, liked to travel, and liked their lifestyle the way it was.

Other reasons why people don't have kids are due to: Increased education, which requires women to stay in school for longer periods of time, often through traditional childbearing years; workforce participation, where if you are too busy working, you are less likely to have children; more effective birth control; economic uncertainty, the fact that women are increasingly deciding to postponing marriage and childbirth, and circumstantial—just didn't meet the right person or infertility issues.

In Laura Scott's book, *Two is Enough*, she shares research that was conducted by sociologists Jean Veevers and Sharon Houseknecht in the 1980s, which explains the motivations for people to choose a childfree lifestyle. Veever's research found that her voluntarily childless subjects felt that parenthood would limit or compromise more desirable life options. And, in Houseknecht's research, where she reviewed 29 studies of the voluntarily childless, she found that both men and women agreed that the most common reason to not have children was "freedom from the responsibility of child rearing and freedom to be spontaneous and to pursue activities they believed offered a greater opportunity for self-fulfillment."[6]

Another reason that childfree couples shared with me is that they didn't want their relationship to change. They liked what they had and felt that having children would hurt or ruin their relationship. Many even told me that they knew of studies that showed that childfree couples where happier than those couples with children.

As I mentioned in the Relationship Section, marital satisfaction for couples drops significantly – anywhere from 60 to 90% after the birth of their first child. And, a 2005 study by researchers at Vanderbilt and Florida State University reports a higher rate of depression among parents than among nonparents. Parents experience lower levels of emotional well-being, less frequent positive emotions, and more frequent negative emotions than their childless peers. No group of parents—married, single, step, or empty nest—reported a greater emotional well-being than people who never had children.[7]

Interviews

People have their own reasons for not wanting to have children. Robert, a 60-year-old freelance writer, told me that the reasons he didn't want to have children were that he came from a dysfunctional family, liked his current life and freedom, and really doesn't like to be around people much. He told me that he was going to be very honest with me and tell me things that no one else has the guts to tell me, such as: "When I go to restaurants and see children, I don't want to sit near them." Or, "When kids cry, I just want them to shut up. I know some people think it's beautiful, but I can't stand it." And, "Kids just bother me. I think when they are 7 or 8, they are more tolerable, but babies are annoying."

Susan, a 48-year-old college administrator, told me that if she was never against having children, but she said she really didn't want to do it alone. She said she never met the "right" person and just continued living her life and working. She immensely enjoys her job, in which she interacts with many people, travels internationally, and spends time with her nieces and nephews during family holidays. She is satisfied with her life.

Paul, a 32-year-old Ivy League MBA, told me that he just wasn't interested in having children. "All that kid stuff is not interesting to me. I prefer adult environments and adult conversations. I don't have the patience for children. Plus, my sister has 6 kids, so I feel I don't need to have any."

Scott, a 34-year-old banker, says that he knew when he was in high school he didn't want to have children. He said, "Life looked easier without them, and I have other interests that I want to pursue. I also want to make money so I can enjoy my life. Kids tend to reduce savings and time that I can spend on my work, travel, eating out, and socializing.

Ashley, a 24-year-old law student, said that she doesn't see herself having children at this point. She says she grew up in a large family and took care of many of her brothers and sisters and felt that she already helped raise a few kids. "I feel that I spent much of my childhood helping raise my siblings, so I really don't have a desire to have any of my own. I know how much work it takes and I'd rather pursue my own interests at this point."

Not fitting in

Whenever I interviewed people who didn't have children, they complained about not being accepted or included in this "child-centric" or "family-focused" society that we live in. They said they felt overlooked or looked down upon. Women said that they felt judged by others because they decided not to have children.

Yet, the people I interviewed who had children and families said that they felt that our society has become less family-friendly, citing restaurants and movie theaters that boycott children and the increased costs for education and other necessities for children. These parents said they feel that they are the outsiders and burden to society because they decided to have kids.

It's amazing that we live in the same society, with both groups feeling alienated. Can it be that we are so used to our own point of view that we can't relate to the experience of another? Why do the childfree and the people with children have to be at odds?

The most common comment I've heard made by parents about childfree people is that childfree people aren't able to relate to parents because they don't know what it's like to be a parent.

And having been a childfree person longer than I've been a parent, I can say I don't think childfree people mind that other people have kids as long as parents are being responsible in raising them.

It just comes down to respecting the choices and decisions of each other and realizing that we all have different preferences in how we live our lives.

QUESTION:

A distant family member who has a 5-year-old child accidently died and unbeknownst to you, has listed you as the guardian. What would you do?

12. WILL I REGRET IT IF I DO HAVE KIDS OR IF I DON'T?

There are many people who do not regret having or not having kids. However, there are some that do. Before I explain some of the reasons people regret that they have or do not have kids, I want to explain some of the new research and thinking from scientists that may explain why people may have more regrets now in today's society and also how our mind helps us adjust to new situations to help us maintain a level of happiness.

Having too many options in life may cause regrets, either way

In Barry Schwartz's book, *The Paradigm of Choice*, which I mentioned in the beginning of this book, he explained how having too many choices causes people confusion and decision paralysis – since having more options to choose from may make it difficult to choose at all. One reason for the paralysis is that people fear and anticipate regret. Then, when people overcome their paralysis and make a decision, they are less satisfied with the result of that decision. The dissatisfaction occurs because it is easy for people to imagine another scenario that may have been better, and that imagined scenario subtracts from the enjoyment of the decision that was made, even if it was good.

Another reason people feel dissatisfied with decisions they make is due to opportunity cost. Opportunity cost is the benefit lost when pursuing a particular choice—it's the other alternative that you didn't take. The way you value things depends on what you compare them to—which is what you gave up in order to make the selection you did. You imagine the options that you may have missed and compare them to your current situation. That alternative you didn't take may have a lot more attractive features, which will make what you're doing seem less attractive. For example, if you choose to have children, the natural tendency will be for you to compare your situation with those who doesn't have children. And people without children will compare their situation to that of people who do have children.

Having more choices and options has also increased our expectations. Because we have more options, our expectations about how good our choice is have increased. With more options and freedom to choose, we think our choice will be perfect. We compare what we got to our expectations. But, when what we get doesn't meet our expectations, we will be less satisfied with the results, even though the results were good.

When we have more choices, but become less happy with the outcomes, we blame ourselves for this unhappiness. This occurs because people believe they are responsible and should be able to figure out the best scenario for themselves. We think there are no excuses for failure. Schwartz believes that depression and suicide are on the increase in industrialized countries because too many choices and options lead to disappointing experiences because standards are so high. When they have to explain their experiences to themselves, they think they are somehow at fault—they didn't make the "right" choice.

Regrets people have when having children

People I interviewed voiced that one of their concerns about deciding whether or not to have a child was a fear that they'd regret having them. According to my research, there are people who never regretted having children and then there were some who did. The regrets parents mentioned were situational, developmental, involved their relationship with their child, the child's personality, and how their child turned out. Overall, most of these regrets were just temporary, due to the difficulty of the situation at the time.

A situational regret is one that arises in a parent during day-to-day living with their child, but is due to nothing the child has done. The parent truly loves their child, but the parent is feeling overburdened, unhappy, just not "into" being a parent. In this case, it's usually an indication that something is out of balance or a need is not being met in the parent's life. Are they working too much, do they not have time for themselves, is there something that they want to pursue or study but feel that they can't because they have to care for their children, or are they stumped by a developmental issue with their child that they don't know how to deal with? When people become parents, it's somehow assumed that they should have all the answers. But, unfortunately, not many parents have studied child development or child psychology. The feeling of regret can be an indication to take the time to see what's going on in a parent's life so they can make adjustments. It doesn't have to be an ongoing feeling of regret; it is the opportunity to see what isn't working and make changes.

Some parents have shared that they may have regretful feelings when their children were in certain stages of development. They have mentioned colicky babies that pushed them to their limit, curious and rambunctious toddlers that didn't listen, or defiant teenagers who started asserting their independence. Raising kids is a process. They grow and change, and each stage causes the parents to possibly adjust and discover new ways to deal with this developing person. If a stage is difficult, it's probably time to get information about what's going on so you can have a better understanding.

I've interviewed mothers who told me how difficult it was to get through the teen years with their daughters. Those were the times they felt regret. Other parents told me they felt frustrated because they couldn't connect with their children and felt that their children didn't listen to them.

Some parents told me that they just couldn't relate to their child, that the child was very different from them and it was hard to connect. This made it difficult to have a relationship, and some regretted having children in this case. Another told me that she just didn't like her child's personality and temperament. "She was just difficult for me to relate to." This mother was more of a homebody who liked to sew, and her daughter was an outgoing tom boy who loved sports. In these cases, regret doesn't have to remain. There are courses of action that can be tried to remedy the situation and try to improve the relationship, if the parent chooses to do so. Therapy can help parents understand their children better, and even going together can improve the relationship.

Another time parents regretted having children was when the child ultimately did something to harm themselves and/or others. Parents whose children became drug addicts, experienced mental illness, or committed suicide felt badly that their child suffered so much. And, it hurt them deeply to watch it happen, no matter how much they tried to help. In those cases, parents said that although they loved their children, they regretted that their child had to experience so much pain, and some still blamed themselves for their child's actions or death. Other parents felt remorse and regret when their child hurt someone or ended up in jail. They often wonder what they did wrong.

Regrets people have when they don't have children

For the people who decided not to have children, many of those that I interviewed didn't have any regrets, while only a few mentioned that they did.

Those who had regrets wanted children but couldn't due to fertility problems, and explained how they needed to go through a mourning process to overcome their loss. Another woman mentioned her regret was missing out on a life experience that was important to her. It was the experience itself – of giving birth and raising a child, of having that intimate experience of nurturing another human being. However, she only wanted to have a child if she married and hasn't done so.

In Sylvia Ann Hewlett's book, *Creating A Life: Professional Women and the Quest for Children*, 2002, she surveyed 1,658 high-achieving women and found that 40% were still childless at age 45. Her book focused on childless females who wanted children but had postponed childbearing because of career demands or lack of opportunity. Some expressed regret about the choices they made, but their regret—or more like dissatisfaction—wasn't just about not having children. They were dissatisfied about the lack of options available to them. Those lack of options caused by the harsh realities of biology, economics, workplace policies, time, money, and the availability of suitable partners. But, somehow the book was interpreted as childlessness leads to regret.

Those childfree people who still wanted to be involved with children found ways to do so through work, family, friends, or organizations. Not having children didn't mean they isolated themselves from kids.

I didn't find any studies that show that childfree people regret not having children.

And, most of the childfree people I spoke to didn't have regrets about not having children. Many said they were happy with their jobs and relationships or marriages. They usually enjoyed their freedom and independence.

Regrets may not last, or how our brain helps us stay happy

For those of you who are concerned about regretting having children or not having children, you need to know that for the most part, your brain will automatically help you adjust your level of happiness to whatever situation you find yourself in. So no matter which option you choose, you can adjust.

In Daniel Gilbert's book, *Stumbling on Happiness*, the Harvard psychology professor explains how our brain synthesizes happiness for different experiences we have. He says that our brains have a" psychological immune system"—a cognitive unconscious process—that helps us change the views of the world so we can feel better about the situation we find ourselves in. He says that we think that happiness is something that can be found outside of us by the experiences we live. But, in reality, we take in the experience and situation and our brain synthesize it so that we find happiness in it.

In Gilbert's 2004 TED talk, "Why Are We Happy?," he gives examples of four people who experienced what we'd think were unlucky or tragic experiences. Jim Write, a former democratic congressman, lost everything in the 90s due to Newt Gingrich and a book scandal. Yet, Write claims he is so much better off. Another man was freed after being wrongly accused and spending 37 years in a Louisiana jail. Yet, after he was released, he said it was a glorious experience. Pete Best, the first Beatle drummer before Ringo, said he was happier now than if he was ever with the Beatles.[1] When people hear these people profess that they are better off now, they don't believe them.

To understand why people can't believe that these people would be happy for suffering setbacks or not getting what they want, you need to understand that there are two types of happiness. One is natural happiness, which is the result of getting something you want. The other type of happiness is synthetic happiness, which is what we make when we don't get what we want. Although we can feel good in both situations, when we hear that someone says they are happy when they don't get what they want, it just seems like it's of less quality.

Yet, synthetic happiness is every bit as real and enduring as the happiness you feel when you get what you were aiming for. This occurs because all claims of happiness are from your point of view. Your unique collection of past experiences serves as how you interpret and evaluate your current experience. And although you think you can remember what you said and did in the past, it is very unlikely that you can precisely resurrect your past experience and evaluate it as you would have back then.

Once we have an experience, we cannot simply set it aside and see the world as we would have seen it had the experience never existed. Our experiences instantly become part of the lens through which we view our entire past, present, and future, and like any lens, they shape and distort what we see. The more recent experience colors your evaluation of your past experience, leaving them unable to say with certainty how they truly feel about their past.

So if you have a child, there is a good chance that you will adjust to your situation and be positive about it. And, if you decide not to have a child, there is a good chance that you will adjust to your situation and be positive about it.

QUESTION:

The accomplishment approach: Put together a list of things you'd like to do or accomplish during our lifetime. This type of exercise can be helpful when you are at a crossroads and trying to find direction or increase inspiration for moving forward in life.

The deathbed approach: If you can imagine that you are 95-years-old and are on your death bed, reflecting back upon your life, what are those experiences you would have wanted to have? Would you have wanted to give birth, be a mother, or have children in your life?

Top Twelve Questions to Help You Decide Whether or Not You Want a Child

Caveat: These questions are purely hypothetical. Some may be uncomfortable to think about because of the severity of the situations I ask you to imagine yourself in. The purpose of asking these questions are to help you get clear about which of the 12 Factors are important to you in your decision to have a child. There are no "right" or "wrong" answers. Everybody has their own life and opinion. Try to not over think these questions and just say the first thing that comes to mind. The most important thing to remember about making your decision to have a child is to do what's right for you and your relationship.

1. **Population/Environmental concerns:** In five years, through technology and progressive legislation, the world is on track to remedy most of its population and environmental issues. Would you consider having a

child if you knew that the world's problems would be improving or were remedied?

2. **Finances:** If you had $2 million in the bank and no financial concerns, would you consider having a child?

3. **Health & Body:** If your significant other could get pregnant and give birth (even if he is male – just use your imagination), would you be more likely to have a child?

4. **Significant Other:** If your significant other or partner happened to die suddenly, would you regret that you didn't have a child with them, or would you be content to know that at least you had the opportunity to share their time and experiences with them while they were here?

5. **Emotional Maturity:** Pick a friend you like and admire and ask yourself if you think they are ready to have a child. Write down their qualities that make them emotionally "ready" or not. Sometimes looking at someone else helps us identify and articulate the qualities we think are important in being able to take care of a child. Now compare yourself to the list you just created. Do you have those qualities?

Or, ask a friend whose opinion you trust and ask them to tell you honestly if they think you are ready to have a child. Then ask them to tell you why or why not.

Or, if someone told you that you were NOT emotionally mature enough to have a child, what would be your response?

6. **Parenting:** Think back to how you were parented and identify what you liked and didn't like? If your imaginary child asked you to explain to them why you had them, what would you tell them?

7. **Career or Stay-at-home?:** This question tries to assess how much your career/job means to you and how flexible you are with taking time off or taking another path. If you got fired from your job right now, how would you feel about it? Is the job something that you are passionate about? Or do you think that you will look for another job in the same industry? Or are you a bit relieved that you no longer "have to go back to that place?"

8. **Childcare:** If you knew that you had an exceptional childcare provider that would help you after you had a child, and would be there to give you a break when you needed it, would you be more likely to have a child?

9. **Relationships**

   A.   Partner: What's the longest you've ever went without sex as an adult? Could you go without sex for six months if you had to?

   B.   Family: What are your expectations with family involvement and help? How involved would you want them to be? What is realistic? If your mother said that she'd help you watch your infant for five days, would that be a "good" thing?

   C.   Friends: Do you have a friend who's had a child? How did your relationship change? Usually common experiences join people together. Reflect upon your life and the friends you've had and you currently have. Where and how did you meet them? What if all your friends disappeared tomorrow? Poof! How would you cope?

    D. Co-workers: What would you do in these situations, when you have a meeting to attend in 30 minutes?

- The school calls to tell you that your child has a scraped his leg, a fever, or is vomiting?
- Your pet that you love dearly, cut itself or is sick and throwing up?
- Your boyfriend or girlfriend was just in a car accident, and although doesn't need to go to the hospital is quite shaken up?

10. **Benefits of having a child**: Think of 3 benefits or "good reasons" to have a child. If you can't think of any, it may be an indication that you are only focusing on the negative. As with most things in life, there are positive and negative sides to every circumstance – even having a child. And, if you are being objective, you probably can figure out aspects for both sides of the situation.

11. **Childfree type**: A distant family member who has a 5-year-old child accidently died and, unbeknownst to you, has listed you as the guardian. What would you do?

12. **Regrets:**

    The accomplishment approach: Put together a list of things you'd like to do or accomplish during our lifetime. This type of exercise can be helpful when you are at a crossroads and trying to find direction or increase inspiration for moving forward in life.

    The deathbed approach: If you can imagine that you are 95-years-old and on your death bed, and were reflecting back upon your life, what are those experiences you would have wanted to have? Would you have wanted to give birth, be a mother, or have children in your life?

STEP THREE:

MAKING YOUR DECISION

STEP 3 - MAKING YOUR DECISION

"Just trust yourself, then you will know how to live."
– Goethe

In this final step, you finally make a decision. In earlier sections, I mentioned how brain research has shown that easy decisions should be made with the frontal cortex, with rationality. Big decisions about your likes and life need to be made with your emotions, your gut, or your intuition.

As the scientist Ap Dijksterhuis advised, "Use your conscious mind to acquire all the information you need for making a decision. But, don't try to analyze the information with your conscious mind. Instead, go on a vacation while your unconscious mind digests it. Whatever your intuition then tells you is almost certainly going to be the best choice."

Up until this point, we have been in an information collection phase, using our conscious minds to acquire all the relevant information we need – both personal and factual. Now I am going to explain ways to let your unconscious mind digest the information you have learned. Then I'll discuss ways to tap into your intuition to give you an indication of your decision. And, finally, I will give you a question to help you figure out your decision.

1: WHY INTUITION IS IMPORTANT

Intuition: *The act or faculty of knowing or sensing without the use of rational processes.*

Intuition is the ability to get a sense, vision, or feeling about someone or something. Intuition communicates with us through symbols, feelings, and emotions. It usually does not speak to us in clear language. We all have intuition. We are born with it. We use it as children; we do not know any better. We go on our instinct or gut. But as we grow older and our rational and reasonable mind develops, we lose touch with our intuition. We forget about it. But there are things to do to get more in touch with your intuition.

2: BODY COMPASS

One method that some chiropractors and life coaches use involves tapping into your body's inner knowledge about your preferences. For chiropractors, this approach is called applied kinesiology. They use it in diagnosing different ailments in their clients, from aches and pains to food sensitivities. Life coaches refer to it as the body compass and have used a form of this to help their clients get out of their heads so they can gain insight for their career or life goals. The idea behind looking to the body for insight is that it is believed that your body contains the inner knowledge about what is good and bad for it. By accessing that knowledge, you can get emotional and intuitive guidance to questions you have.

One commonly known and basic applied kinesiology test is the arm-pull-down test, or "Delta test." A subject holds his arm out in front of him. Another person asks the subject a question. The subject doesn't answer the question; instead, the person asking the question exerts force on the subject's arm. If the arm holds strong, then the answer is yes and means that the option is beneficial to the subject. If the arm weakens and gives way, it means that option isn't good for the subject.

Using the Delta Test in gaging your interest in having a child, you would hold your arm straight out in front of your body. A friend would ask you if you want to have a child. You don't have to answer the question. Instead, your friend would push down on your arm. If your arm is firm, it means that you are interested in having a child. If your arm gives way, it means you aren't interested in having a child.

The body compass approach is another way to access the body's inner wisdom. Usually a person starts in a standing position to calibrate which movement means "yes" and "no." They have their eyes closed and are told to relax. Then a friend or helper tells them to ask their bodies, "Please show me a clear sign for yes." Then wait to see what happens. Many times, a person will lean forward slightly, but there could be other sensations in other parts of the body. Then the friend or helper tells them to ask themselves, "Please show me a clear sign for no." Then they wait to see what happens. Many times, the person will lean backward an inch or so. If the person just stands straight, it means they need more information or need to ask the body again. Once the person knows what their yes and no are, someone can ask them a question, such as, "Do I want to have a child?" and see which way they lean.

For example, let's say that a person leans forward for "yes" and leans back on their heels for "no." When their friends asks them, "Do you want to have a child?" and they lean forward, that is an indication that they do. If they lean back, it is an indication that they do not.

3: QUIETING THE MIND

At this point, it is important that you do not analyze the information you learned and that you do not keep thinking about the question. Here are some suggestions to get out of your head:

1. Do something. Get moving. Get physical. Exercise. Do yoga. Play a sport. Engage in an activity that causes you to focus and pay attention to your physical movement so you can't and won't be able to think of anything else.

2. Meditation is a way to quiet the mind. It's not easy for everyone to do, but it teaches you how to learn how to observe the chatter that goes on in our minds. It helps you get beyond your thoughts to the more authentic you.

3. Find something that engrosses you and gets you in the flow. When we do things that absorb our attention, we aren't preoccupied by busy thoughts or over-thinking. Find things you love to do and do them.

4. Do things that give you pleasure. Make a list of things that you really enjoy doing, and once a day, do at least one of those.

4: TRUSTING FATE OR DESTINY

Some people believe there are forces beyond their control – a higher power – a god, that influences or guides their lives. Some people believe in fate and destiny. Some people look for coincidences to give them an indication that they are on the right track.

When I was interviewing women for my book, I heard many "accidental" or "surprise" pregnancy stories that were, "just meant to be." I would sit and listen to their stories and quietly think to my rational self that these women were just trying to justify their experience by explaining their irresponsibility with birth control. Maybe now because I know how the brain works, this could be how their prefrontal cortex was rationalizing their experience. I also know from my own experience that maybe these decisions were made at the subconscious, and maybe even spiritual, level.

The OB-GYN

One of my all-time favorite interviews was with an OB-GYN I met at a Planned Parenthood Fundraiser. The irony of her story always brings a smile to many people who hear it. A friend of mine who knew I was researching this book asked me to come to the fundraiser and introduced me to Margo, who volunteered her services at a local clinic. Margo told me her story. She shared that several years back, when she was in her early forties and was still childless, she thought that maybe she wasn't meant to have children, although she always wanted them. She said she had been busy building her practice and never met the right guy. She told me she attended the same fundraiser, only several years prior. There she said she met a man and they had a fabulous night, which resulted in what she thought was a one-night-stand, even though they did exchange cards. Several weeks later, Margo learned she was pregnant.

She said, "I was embarrassed and laughed at myself because I had quite a few patients who would come to me pregnant and tell me they didn't know how it happened because they were on the pill. I always thought they were lying and that they didn't take their pills properly. " But she said she was also on the pill and got pregnant.

It didn't take Margo long to decide that she was going to keep the baby. She said, "I was in my early 40's, my practice was thriving, so money wasn't an issue, and I always wanted a

252

child. I really felt this was meant to be. I felt my baby was a gift from God."

Being a mature adult, Margo called the father of the child to tell him the news. She said she didn't want anything from him, but out of fairness, since she was going to keep and raise the child, she thought he'd want to know. The man, being in his early 50s and never married, was surprised to learn the news and said he'd like to be involved in the child's life.

As Margo finished her story, she stepped aside and introduced me to the father of her child. They didn't marry, but moved in together as a couple and are raising their six-year-old-little girl.

The women who would never have children

A 38-year-old woman with two sons I interviewed told me that she was told that she wouldn't be able to have children. Dahlia was told this news when she was in her late teens because she had serious issues with her menstrual cycle. Her father was a surgeon, so he made sure she had the best medical care and advice. She said she resigned her mind and life to that fact. She ended up meeting a boy in college, who was fine with the fact that he may not be able to have children, and they ended up marrying a year or two out of college. Nine years later, Dahlia learned she was pregnant. "I was shocked," she said. "I never thought this would happen. But I took it as a sign that I was supposed to have this baby." Dahlia had a baby boy and then a few years later another gave him a brother.

My story

In my case, I was never interested in motherhood for a variety of reasons. My childhood experiences gave me a negative perception of mothering and caring for children. I always thought I couldn't have a child because I had horrible menstrual cramps that landed me in the emergency room on several occasions and required me to take morphine for my pain. And, because I focused my energies toward school and work, I really couldn't relate to the world of kids and moms. It was a foreign land to me.

I always wondered if something was wrong with me because I didn't want children. And I was with someone who was kind and loving, which made me doubt my own thoughts about not having children. So to resolve my confusion, I spent time learning about myself, as well as interviewing others, to see if I could gain some insight to what I really wanted.

To help me on my quest, a college friend organized a group interview session for me in the Midwest with several women who had four or more kids (the highest amount was a mom with nine), so I could ask them questions. If I wanted to know what motivated people to want and have kids, my friend thought, these ladies would be able to tell me. The session was informative, and I left having much respect for these women and a deep appreciation for taking so much time to share their intimate thoughts and feelings about motherhood, their children, and their relationships.

After the interview session, one of my many cousins took me to a party where she said she had a surprise for me. She informed me that a very good psychic would be there, and she thought it a good idea that I see him. Although I was skeptical, I went into the den where Kevyn, the psychic, was performing his magic. He was a young kid, about 20 or 21 years old, with a bit of acne. I thought I'd humor him. The first thing he said to me after laying out the tarot cards was, "Tell me about the book you are writing." I was a bit impressed, but challenged him throughout the session. He said many interesting and accurate things. At the end of my session, he asked me if there was anything else I wanted to know. So, although I wasn't sure

I really wanted to know, I did ask him if I was going to have kids. And he quickly and matter-of-factly said, "Of course. You're going to have a boy and a girl." When I asked him when, he said, "Within two years." I told him, "That's not going to happen." He rolled his eyes and said, "That's your destiny." I paid him and left thinking that was a waste of money.

A few months later, I was seeing a doctor to deal with my menstrual cramps. She told me if I just had a baby, my cramps would go away. I told her I wasn't going to have a baby just to get rid of cramps. Over the next three months, she performed different tests and in the end, she scheduled a laparoscopy. She warned me that if she found tumors or other major problem, there may be a chance she'd have to perform a hysterectomy during the procedure. She said she was telling me this now because she wanted me to understand that I wouldn't be able to have children. I said I was fine with that.

About a week before my surgery, the doctor's assistant called me to tell me that the doctor had a family emergency in India and that we had to cancel my surgery. She said the doctor would return in two months. I told the assistant that once the doctor was back in the country to call me to reschedule. I could wait a few months. Well, in two months, I was pregnant—nine months after Kevyn, the psychic, predicted. And, I did have a boy. And, I have no more menstrual cramps. Miracles all around.

And, now like many of the women that I interviewed, I can also say, "It was meant to be."

I want to share these stories because I think that sometimes we can think and think and think about making a decision, and sometimes our subconscious knows we are ready. I was ready. I had done so much research and interviewing that I was pretty comfortable. And, my husband and I talked about so many different aspects that we got to the

255

point that if I got pregnant we'd be fine and if we didn't we'd be fine. Also, I was more aware of how I was going to treat my child differently than the way I was raised. But maybe because of my fear of pregnancy and childbirth, I was hesitant.

For those of you who are tired of over-analyzing your choice, but are mature and open enough to trust God, fate, destiny – whichever you prefer – this is a valid choice. You are making the decision to let things happen, if they are meant to be.

5: MAKING YOUR DECISION

At this point, we want to tap into your emotional brain to make a decision. To do this, we have to do it in such a way so we don't get your rational brain involved. Once you start thinking, you can get distracted from your true feelings. The best way to tap into your emotional brain is for someone to ask you a question when you aren't mentally prepared for it. There needs to be an element of surprise or an unplanned approach. It's not easy to do to yourself. Here are some suggestions for you to access your emotional brain:

1. Enlist a friend to help you. To tap into your emotional brain, you need access it without engaging your rational mind. It is best if you are feeling happy and content with life. When you aren't expecting it, have a friend ask you if you want to have a child. By asking you when you are in a positive, happy frame of mind and the question comes to you when you least expect it, your response will probably be very accurate for you.

2. You can also go to my website, www.annmeredith.net, and select the tab, "Make your decision." You will give me your e-mail address and fill out a little section about your situation. Then, in a week or two, when

256

you least suspect it, I will send you a provoking question to get a visceral reaction from you that will give you clear indication whether or not you want a child.

6: FEELING GOOD ABOUT YOUR DECISION

By reading this book, you have spent a considerable amount of time learning about yourself and the various factors people consider when deciding whether to have a child. You have probably done more than most people on the planet. For that effort alone, you can feel that whatever decision you make will have been done thoroughly.

Also brain research has shown that for most of us, once we make our decision, our brains tend to develop reasoning to justify our decisions. So whatever you decide, you will be able to explain it so that it fits into your life story.

There are also some decision-making realities to keep in mind about any decision you make:

1. You can always find regrets.
2. You'll never have 100% of the information
3. A decision to pursue one goal may require you to forgo others.
4. There are no right or wrong decisions or choices in life.
5. Sometimes life is not in our control, and we don't always get everything we want, so the secret is to enjoy what we have.

One woman I spoke to, who was in her early 40s and didn't have children, told me that she felt badly because she didn't really take the time to make a conscious decision. She was in a relationship and happily leading a busy life. But, she felt that by not making a deliberate decision, she felt irresponsible and incomplete. That there was an emptiness or a void signifying to her that something was not resolved.

She shared with me what did end up making her feel better about NOT deciding. She said that one of her friends with kids told her that having a child is not something we all get to choose. Life doesn't work that way for many of us. Her friend told her stories of other friends who desperately wanted children, but surprisingly couldn't get pregnant, and others who did not want to have a child, then surprisingly get pregnant. Sometimes, life doesn't give us want we want. When she realized that making a deliberate decision doesn't mean we get what we want, and that the decision to have a child is not always in our control, she had the understanding she needed to move forward.

ACKNOWLEDGEMENTS

This book would not be here if all the women and men I interviewed weren't willing to share their stories with me. I have spent the past 10 years interviewing people about their decision to have children. I'd like to thank them for taking the time, sometimes hours and days, out of their busy schedules and lives to honestly share their experiences with me and permit me to ask very personal questions about their thoughts and feelings about having children and how they came to their decision whether to have them or not. Because of all of you, I was better prepared when I finally did have a child.

I also want to thank the friends and family who patiently listened to me throughout the years as I talked about, "THE BOOK," and encourage me to finish it. Thank you, Andi Armaganean, Jose Cerezo, Jen & John Curran, Alicia Fitts, Rob Friedman, Keith Gontarek, Beth Griffith, Elaine Hagan, Dr. Lara Honos-Webb, Randy James, David Knoll, Maria Kroninger, Dr. Sharon Lamm-Hartmann, Elizabeth Major, Mike Mall, Larry Massey, Jamie Mayer, Linda Pearson, Michelle Pujol, Jennifer Robertson, Lisa Romish, Christy Ross, Robin Rothwell, Dawn Rutkowski, Loretta & Paul Saracino, Heather Smith, Alan Sparks, Jackie Sullivan, Dana Teegardin, PJ Thomas, Alex Walters, Robin West, and Christine Williams for all your support.

I'd also like to thank Martha Beck, for encouraging me to live my life and Sarah Mclean, who taught me how to meditate.

A special thank you goes to Alicia Dunams for helping me accomplish my lifetime dream of writing this book. If it weren't for her deadlines and the editing help of Patti McKenna and Rie Langdon, this book may still be in my head.

And, I can't forget Dr. Beth Halbert, Cheryl Mitchell, Heidi Sloss, and Dora Wallace, who all experienced this writing journey with me.

Another thank you goes to all those wonderful strangers who gave me encouraging smiles as I was a new mother learning my way in the world. To those who opened doors when my hands were full or helped me carry bags to my car. To those little acts of kindness that gave me hope about humanity. All those times I felt alone and wondered, "How do people get through this?" it seems that someone would pop into my life and show me how.

And most importantly, I would like to say a huge thank you to my husband, Jim. If it weren't for him I would have had no reason to write this book. I thank you for always being supportive of my interests, no matter how bizarre, and thank you for encouraging me every time I wanted to give up.

Lastly, I want to thank my sweet boy, Ansen, who has helped me learn more about life and myself than any other adventure I've pursued so far. I am so excited to see where life takes us.

RESOURCES AND REFERENCES

Foundations for making a Good Decision

1 National Center for Health Statistics Report, Aug. 2009.

2 Center of Disease Control's Vital Signs Report, Apr. 2011.

3 Ibid.

4 Daily Women's Health Policy Report, National Partnership for Women & Families, Advisory Board.

5 Ibid.

6 National Center for Health Statistics, Mar. 2011.

7 Ibid.

8 National Center for Health Statistics, Aug. 2010.

9 National Vital Statistics System, Dec. 2010.

10 National Center for Health Statistics, Mar. 2011.

11 Pew Research Center

12 The Census Bureau's Current Population Survey.

13 National Survey of Family Growth, 2006-2008, Center for Disease Control, National Center for Health Statistics.

14 Sheena Iyengar, PhD, and Mark Lepper, Ph, Journal of Personality and Social Psychology (JPSP, Vol. 79, No. 6)

15 Henshaw, Stanley K., "Unintended Pregnancy in the United States," Family Planning Perspectives, Vol. 30(1): 24-29 & 46, Jan/Feb 1998.

16 "Facts on Induced Abortion In the United States," Guttmacher Institute, August 2011, www.guttmacher.org

1 How We Decide," Jonah Lehrer, p. 98

2 How We Decide," Jonah Lehrer, p.

3 Walsh D. why do they act that way? A survival guide to the adolescent brain for you and your teen. New York: Free Press 2004.

4 Wilson, Timothy and Schooler, Jonathan W., "Thinking Too Much: Introspection Can Reduce the Quality of Preferences and Decisions", Journal of Personality and Social Psychology, Vol. 60(2), Feb. 1991, P. 181-192.

5 Miller, George A. (1956). "The magical number seven, plus or minus two: some limits on our capacity for processing information". Psychological Review 63 (2): 81–97.

6 Ap Dijkisterhuis, Maarten W. Bos, Loran F. Nordgren and Rick B. van Baaran, "On Making the Right Choice: The Deliberation-Without-Attention Effect." Science, 17 Feb. 2006, Vol. 311 no. 5763 pp. 1005-1007.

1 Gilbert, Daniel, "Stumbling on Happiness" Alfred A. Knoph, New York, 2006, Kindle, p. 544.

2 "Dan Gilbert Asks: Why are we happy? TED Conference, TED2004, www.TED.com.

1 Ap Dijksterhuis

Step 1 – It's All About You

1 Hofberg, Kris~t~ina and Ward, Mark, "Tokophobia: A Profound Dread and Avoidance of Childbirth (When Pathological Fear Effects the Consultation), Psychological Challenges in Obstetrics and Gynecology, Springer, London, 2007, p. 167-168.

2 Nicholas, Sadie, "Are you a tokophobic? The Women who are too terrified to give birth," Daily Mail, The United Kingdom, 27 October 2007.

1 "Gene May Be Clue to Nature of Nurturing," The New York Times, 26 July 1996.

2 Bakermans-Kranenburg, Marian J. and van Ijzendoorn, Marinus H., "Oxytocin receptor (OXTR) and serotonin transporter (5-HTT) genes associated with observed parenting," Oxford University Press, 2008

3 "Effects of maternal behavior induction and pup exposure on neurogenesis in adult, virgin female rats," Furuta, Miyako and Bridges, Robert S., Brain Research Bulletin, Vol. 80, Issue 6, 16. Dec. 2009, Pages 408-413.

4 Parker-Pope, Tara; "Maternal Instinct is Wired Into the Brain," The New York Times, 7 March 2008.

5 Pikul, Corrie, "The Clock-Watcher; How do you know when –or if- you should have a baby?, Elle , May 2011, p. 164-166.

6 6 Pope, Sam, "What makes us maternal?", Babyworld,uk.co,
http://www.babyworld.co.uk/features/community_stories/maternal_instinct_1.asp

7 Ibid.

1 Cohn, D'Vera, "The New Demography of American Motherhood," Pew Research Center, August, 19, 2010, p. 19.

2 Yusuf Al-Qaradawi, Muhammad Saleh Al-Munajjid. "Contraception: Permissible?," IslamOnline.

Step 2 – The Top 12 factors to Consider

1. Population

1 United Nations Development Programme (Sept. 2005) Human Development Report 2005: International Cooperation at a Crossroads-Aid, Trade and Security in an Unequal World.

2 U.S. Census Bureau, International Data Base (IDB), World Population by Age & Sex, Feb. 23, 2011.

3 World Population Prospects; The 2008 Revision, Population Division of the Department of Economic and Social Affairs of the United Nations Secretariat, June, 2009.

4 Ibid.

5 Makcen, Dieirdre "Oh No, we forgot to have children: How declining birth rates are reshaping our society. Allen & Unwin, Australia, 2005.

6 Eberstadt, Nicholas, "The Demographic Future – What Population Growth – and decline – means for the global economy. Foreign Affairs, Wed, Nov/Dec. 2010.

Ibid.

8 Palmer, Brian, "The One Child Fallacy" Slate (USA) Nov. 2, 2010.

9 Ibid.

10 Suzuki, Toru, "Population Policy in Easter Asian Low Fertility Countries," National Institute of Population and Social Security, Tokyo, Japan. Paper presented at the International Population Conference in Marrakech, Morocco, Oct. 2009.

11 "Map: Parenthood Policies in Europe." BBC News, March, 24, 2006, http://news.bbc.co.uk/go/pr/fr/-/2/hi/europe/4837422.stm (accessed on July 22, 2001)

2. Finances

1 Expenditures on Children by Families, 2009. US Dept of Agriculture, Center for Nutrition Policy and Promotion, Pub. No. 1528-2009.

2 Ibid. pg. 10.

3 Ibid. pg. 12.

4 Ibid. pg. 13.

5 "Oh No, We Forgot To Have Children, pg. 69

6 "A Real-Time Look at the Impact of the Recession on Women's Family Planning and Pregnancy Decisions," Guttmacher Institute, September 2009.

7 Centers for Disease Control, National Center for Health Statistics, Vital Statistics, "Table 1-1. Live Births, Birth Rates, and Fertility Rates, by Race: United States, 1909-2000"

8 National Center for Health Statistics, Current Population Survey data by the Council on Contemporary Families, 2008.

9 Steve Martin, Professor of Sociology at the University of Maryland

10 "Do We Need $75,000 a Year to Be Happy?" Time, Sept. 6, 2010.

11 Ibid.

12 Ibid.

13 Ibid.

14

15

16 Borchard, Therese J., "Inside 'This Emotional Life': An Interview With Daniel Gilbert," http://blog.beliefnet.com/beyondblue/2010/01/inside-this-emotional-life-an.html

17 Aknin, Lara, Dunn, Elizabeth, and Norton, Michael, "From Wealth to Well-Being? Money matters, but less than people think," The Journal Of Positive Psychology, 4:6, 523-527. Dec. 2009.

18 American Psychological Association (Aug. 8, 2009), Father-son Team Says Positive Gains Can Be Made in 'Psychological Wealth."

3. Health & Body

1 "'Patient Choice' C-Section Rate Rises 36%: Healthgrade Study," Healthgrades, Golden Colorado, Sept. 12, 2005.

2 American College of Obstetrics and Gynecologist's Committee Opinion, op. cit. note 19, 192.

3 "Fertility Treatment Less Successful After 35," WebMD, July 4, 2006, www.webmd.com.

4 Pregnancy After 35, March of Diimes, May 21, 2008. www.marchofdimes.com.

5 "Pregnancy & Baby Index: Fertility and Conception: Conceiving in your 20s, 30s and 40s. Pregnancy & Baby

6

7 "Family Planning: Are Older Parents Happier Than Younger Parents? www.Babyzone,com

8 "Caesarean versus vaginal birth," A balance view of caesareans, csections.org.

9 "Caesarean versus vaginal birth," A balance view of caesareans, csections.org

10 Ibid.

11 Ibid.

12 "Ibid.

13 "Elective C-section delivery: Does it have a negative effect on breastfeeding?" Zandardo, V. Svegliado G, Cavallin, F, Giustardi A, Cosmi E, Litta P, Treviantuto D. Department of Pediatrics, Padua University School of Medicine, Padua, Italy, December 2010. PubMed, US National Library of Medicine, National Institute of Health

14 Kendall-Takett, Kathleen, "Impact of Negative Birth Experience on Mother/Infant Relationship," The APSAC Advisor, Vol. 7, 9-10: 25-26, 1994.

15 "How Breastfeeding Benefits Mothers," Scientific American, April 30, 2010

16 Ibid.

17 "Longer Maternity Leave Ups Breast-Feeding Rates," Serena Gordon, HealthDay, USNews. May 30, 2011.

18 Paulson JF. Focusing on depression in expectant and new fathers: prenatal and postpartum depression not limited to mothers, Psychiatry Times. 2010;27(2). http://www.psychiatrictimes.com/display-old/article/10168/1519072

19 Postpartum Support International, www.postpartum.net

20 U.S. Obesity Trends, US Center for Disease Control and Prevention. Data from the National Health & Examination Survey,2007 - 2008. http://www.cdc.gov/obesity/data/trends.html

4. Significant Other

1 Livingston, Gretchen, "A Tale of Two Fathers: More are active, but more are absent," Pew Research Center. June. 15, 2011, www.pew.org. http://www.pewtrusts.org/our_work_report_detail.aspx?id=85899360888 (accessed July 25, 2011)

2 Ibid.

3 Ibid.

4 National Survey of Family Growth, 2006-2008, Center for Disease Control, National Center for Health Statistics.

5 National Marriage Project, The State of Our Unions, 2003

6 "Married Couples in Less Than Half of US Households," Yahoo News, May 28, 2011.

7 "Who Marries and When? Age at First Marriage in the United States: 2002, Paula Goodwin, Ph.D.; Brittany Mcgill, M.P.P. and Anjani Chandra, Ph.D. NCHS Data Brief, No. 19, June 2009.

8 25% of Millennials Not Sure About Marriage, Pew Research Center, May 25, 2011.

9 Kidd SA, Eskenazi B. Wyrobek AJ, February 2001, Effects of male age on semen quality and fertility: a review of literature" Gertil. Steril 75 (2): 237-48 www.elsevier.com

10 Dodd, Melinda & Palagano, "Career vs. Paycheck: The Working Mother Report," Working Mother,

11 Richard Fry and D'Vera Cohn, "New Economics of Marriage: The Rise of Wives, " (Washington, D.C.: Pew Research Center, 2010).

12 National Institutes of Health, 1996.

13 "In Troubled Times, Vasectomies Snip and Prosper," Madison Park, CNN, March 24, 2009. Share this on

14 Ibid.

15 Livingston, Gretchen, "A Tale of Two Fathers; More are active, more absent, "Pew Research Center," June 15, 2011.

16 "Grensing-Pophal, "Fathers in the Workplace," Human Resource Executive Online, July, 2, 2010. http://www.hreonline.com/HRE/story.jsp?storyId=465333255 (accessed July 25, 2011).

17 National Center for Health Statistics.

18 US Census Bureau

19 Ricciuti, Henry, "Single Parenthood, Achievement, and Problem Behavior in White, Black, and Hispanic Children," Journal of Educational Research, April 2004, (Vol. 97, No. 4) http://www.tandfonline.com/doi/abs/10.3200/JOER.97.4.196-207.

5. Emotional

1 Bennett, Craig M. and Baird, Abigail A., "Anatomical Changes in the Emerging Adult Brain: A voxel-based morphometry study," Human Brain Mapping, (Vo. 27, Issue 9, pgs 766-777) Sept. 2006.

2 Peck, Ellen and Granzig, Dr. William, "The Parent Test: How to measure and develop your talent for parenthood," G.P. Putnam's Sons, New York, New York, 1978.

3 National Association for Children of Alcoholics

6. Parenting

1 (Albert Bandura 1964) (Holmbeck & Hill, 1988, Offer, Ostrov, & Howard, 1981).

2 (Offer & Schonert-Reichl, 1992).

3 50 Great Myths of Popular Psychology, p. 51-52.

4

5 Nettle, Daniel, "Personality: What Makes You the Way You Are, Oxford University Press, 2007.

6 Steinberg Ph.D, Laurence, "The 10 Basic Principles of Good Parenting," Simon & Shuster, New York, New York, 2004, p13-15.

7 Galinksy, Ellen, "Ask the Children: What America's Children Really Think About Working Parents," William and Morrow, Inc., 1999,

8 Steinberg, Laurence, Ph.D, "The 10 Basic Principles of Good Parenting," Simon & Schuster, New York, New York, 2004.

9 Galinksy, Ellen, "Ask the Children" p. 30-33.

10 NICHD study 860-879

7. Career

1 "Parental Guidance: Sallie Krawcheck on getting to the top as a working mother," The Wall Street Journal, April, 11, 2011, p. R10.

2 Sharon R. Cohany and Emy Sok, "Trends in Labor Force Participation of Married Mothers of Infants, Monthly Review 130, no. 2 (U.S. Bureau of Labor Statistics, 2007) 13.

3 Funk, Cary and Clark, April, "Fewer Mothers Prefer Full-time Work: From 1997 to 2007," PewReserach Center, July 2007.

4 Funk, Cary and Clark, April, "Fewer Mothers Prefer Full-time Work: From 1997 to 2007," PewReserach Center, July 2007.

5 "Good Enough is the New Perfect,"

6 NICHD (National Institute of Child Health and Human Development) Early Child Care Research Network, "The Effects of Child Care on Infant-Mother Attachment Security: Results of the NICHD Study of Early Child Care, " Child Development 68 Number 5 (1997): 860-879.

7 Ibid.

8 Ibid. p. 10.

9 A.S. Fuligni, E. Galinsky, & M. Porter, The Impact of Parental Employment on Children (New York: Families and Work Institute, 1995).

10 Rich, Motoko, "Don't Worry Working Moms," The New York Times, August 3. 2010.

11 Galinksy, Ellen, "Ask the Children: What America's Children Really Think About Working Parents," William Marrow and Company, Inc., 1999, p 9.

12 Parket, Kim, "The Harried Life of the Working Mother," Pew Research Center, October 1, 2009.

13 Kansas State Univeristy (2010, Febrary 18), "People not only judge mothers based on work status, but also judge their kids, ScienceDaily.

14 Hakim, Catherine, Ph.D., Center for Policy Studies

15 Sanberg, Sheryl, Speech at Professional Women of California's Annual Meeting in San Francisco, May 10, 2011.

16 Weiss, Debra Cassens, "About 25 Percent of Lawyer Moms Leave the Workplace, Study Finds," ABA Journal, May 9, 2011.

17 Daunting Task for Mr. Mom: Get a Job, WSJ, Sue Shellnebarger, May 19, 2010

18 Parker, Kim, "The Harried Life of the Working Mother," Pew Research Center, Oct. 1, 2009.

19 Richard Fry and D'Vera Cohn, "New Economics of Marriage: The Rise of Wives, " (Washington, D.C.: Pew Research Center, 2010).

20 Ellicott, Claire, "Businesswomen with nine children claims no woman can succeed without a house-husband," Mail Online, July, 4, 2011.

21 Weiss, Debra Cassens, "These Lawyer Families Are New Twist on Opt-Out Professionals," ABA Journal, Oct. 1, 2009.

8. Childcare

9. Relationships

1 Cowan, C.P. & Cowan, P.A. When partners become parents: The big life change for couples, Mahwah, NJ, Erlbaum (2000).

2 Gottman, J.M, Driver, J. & Tabares, A, "Building the sound marital house: An empirically-derived couple therapy. In A.S. Gurman & N.S. Jacobson, Clinical Handbook of couple therapy (3rd ed., pp. 373-399) New York; Guilford Press (2002)

3 Doss, Brian D.; Rhoades, Galena K.; Stanley, Scott M.; Markman, Howard J.

"The effect of the transition to parenthood on relationship quality: An 8-year prospective study," Journal of Personality and Social Psychology, Vol 96(3), Mar 2009, 601-619.

4 Ibid.

5 Ibid

6 Ibid.

7 Belsky, J, & Hsieh, K, "Patterns of marital change during the early childhood years: Parent personality, coparenting and division-of-labor correlates. Journal of Family Psychology, 12, 511-528 (1998).

8 "As Marriage and Parenthood Drift Apart, Public Is Concerned About Social Impact: Generation Gap in Values, Behaviors," Pew Research Center, July 1, 2007.

9 Byrd, J. et al. "Sexuality During Pregnancy and the Year Postpartum," Journal of Family Practice, 1998, 47(4), p. 305-308.

10 Herbenick, Debby, Ph.D., "Sex After Baby," Men's Health, February 1, 2011.

11 Byrd, J. et al. "Sexuality During Pregnancy and the Year Postpartum," Journal of Family Practice, 1998, 47(4), p. 305-308.

12 Hartmann K, Viswnathan M, Palmieri R, et al, "Outcomes of routine episiotomy: A system review," JAMA, 2005: 293 (17).

13 Weber AM, Meyn L. Episiotomy use in the United States, 1979–1997. Obstet and Gynecol 2002; 100: 1177–82.

14 Webb DA; Culhane J. Hospital variation in episiotomy use and the risk of perineal trauma during childbirth. Birth 2002; 29: 132–6.

15 Berman, Dr. Jennifer, "Why I had an elective c-section," www.bermansexualhealth.com.

16 Smith, Tim W, "American Sexual Behavior: Trends, Socio-Demographic Differences, and Risk Behavior, " National Opinion Research Center, University of Chicago, GSS Topical Report No. 28, March 2006, Version 6. P. 7-8.

17 Blanchflower, D. G. and Oswald, A. J. (2004), Money, Sex and Happiness: An Empirical Study. The Scandinavian Journal of Economics, 106: 393–415. doi: 10.1111/j.0347-0520.2004.00369

18 Buchanan, Ann and Flouri, Erini Ph.D., " University of Oxford, or "Grandma And Grandpa Are Good For Children," ScienceDaily (June 7, 2008).

19 Pollet, Thomas, et al, "Family Ties That Bind: Maternal Grandparents Are More Invovled In The Lives Of Their Grandchildren," Evolutionary Psychology, Dec. 19, 2007

20 Belkin, Lisa, "How Friendships Change After Baby," New York Times, March, 5, 2010.

21 Ibid.

22 Ibid.

10. Benefits

1 Cohn, D'Vera, et. al. "The New Demography of American Motherhood," Pew Research Center, August 19, 2010.

11. Am I the Childfree Type

1 www.childlessbychoiceproject.comm

2 National Center for Health Statistics

3 National Center for Health Statistics

4 Scott, Laura S., "Two is Enough: A Couple's Guide to Living Childless By Choice," Sept. 2009. p. 345.

5 Notkin, Melanie, *The Truth About Childless Women*, Huffington Post, July, 11, 2011

6 Scott, Laura S., "Two is Enough: A Couple's Guide to Living Childless By Choice," Sept. 2009.

7 Evenson, Ranae and Simon, Robin, "Clarifying the Relationship Between Parenthood and Depression," Journal of Health and Social Behavior (2005), Vol. 46; 341-358.

12. Will I Regret my Decision?

1 Gilbert, Dan, "Why Are We Happy," TED Talk, 2004.

http://www.ted.com/talks/lang/eng/dan_gilbert_asks_why_are_we_happy.htm